The Birdkeepers' Guide
COCKATIELS

The Birdkeepers' Guide
COCKATIELS

GREG GLENDELL

T.F.H. Publications, Inc.
One TFH Plaza
Third and Union Avenues
Neptune City, NJ 07753

Printed and bound in China
08 09 10 11 12 1 3 5 7 9 8 6 4 2

Library of Congress Cataloging-in-
Publication Data
Glendell, Greg.
   Cockatiels / Greg Glendell.
      p. cm. — (The birdkeepers' guide)
   Includes index.
   ISBN 978-0-7938-0654-6 (alk. paper)
   1. Cockatiel. I. Title.
   SF473.C6G54 2008
   636.6'8656—dc22
            2008002327

*The Leader in
Responsible Animal
Care for Over 50
Years!*®
www.tfh.com

Greg Glendell BSc (Hons)

Greg Glendell has had a lifelong interest in birds. As an amateur
ornithologist he has carried out fieldwork on bird habitat
requirements and the breeding biology of native British birds.
Following his degree in Environmental Science, which included
coursework on animal and human behavior, he worked in
wildlife conservation. He acquired his first parrot, a blue-fronted
Amazon, in 1986 and this led to him developing a deep interest
in these birds. He has bred parrots but no longer does so as
there is a surplus of these birds in need of good homes. He
keeps several parrots including greys, Amazons, and a Meyer's.
Greg works as the UK's only full-time pet parrot behavioral
consultant and is based in Somerset. You can e-mail Greg at
mail@greg-parrots.co.uk and visit his website: www.greg-
parrots.co.uk <http://www.greg-parrots.co.uk/> for more
details of his consultancy. He is the
author of *Breaking Bad Habits in
Parrots* and the Birdkeepers' Guides
to *African Greys* and *Amazons*.

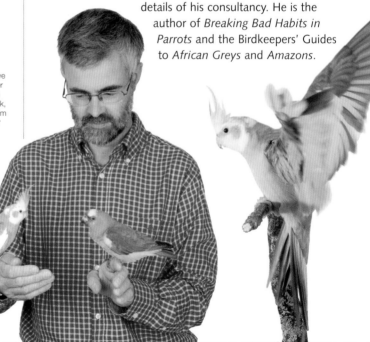

Contents

CHAPTER 1

Origins of the cockatiel

Wild cockatiels are found throughout Australia and are quite common over much of their range. They tend to be found in the interior of the country, rather than near the coast and they are absent from northern Queensland. While cockatiels have been seen in Tasmania, these are believed to be escaped birds rather than wild ones.

⇦ *The cockatiel is found across most of Australia where it prefers an open woodland habitat with gum trees.*

Cockatiels are 12 to 13in (30 to 33cm) long. They are slender, long-tailed birds bigger than a budgerigar. Many captive-bred birds have plumage very different from their wild relatives. The wild cockatiel is gray with large white wing patches which are highly visible when seen in flight. The face is yellow with a large orange-red patch over the ear-coverts and an erectile crest on the head. Unlike most

⇩ *A group of wild cockatiels in Australia. They are usually found in large flocks and are quite common birds throughout the country.*

parrots, adult cockatiels can be sexed on plumage. The "normal" female has fine pale yellow and grey bars on the tail and under the wings and her face is duller than the male's. The plumage difference between the sexes of many captive-bred birds is often not so apparent.

"Little nymphs"

The scientific name of the cockatiel is *Nymphicus hollandicus*. Early European travellers were so taken by the beauty of these birds in flight that they called them "little nymphs" after the beautiful mythical creatures that were reputed to live in woods, groves, and streams. The word "hollandicus" comes from the early name for Australia which was New Holland. These birds are the sole representatives of their genus of *Nymphicus* and there are no very close relatives. There had been some confusion as to which type of parrot-like bird the cockatiel was related to, and it seems its closest relatives are the very large black cockatoos, such as the yellow-tailed black cockatoo and the white-tailed black cockatoo, also found in Australia.

Until the 1960s wild-caught cockatiels were imported from Australia but as they breed freely in captivity, captive populations were soon established in many countries all around the world. Today all cockatiels on sale are captive-bred, and they are very popular pet birds throughout the world.

In the wild, the cockatiel is found in many different types of habitat from open woodland to semi-desert, farmland, and scrub. It is generally found close to a source of water and is common in river valleys. Cockatiels are fast, buoyant flyers and often associate with budgerigars, particularly at sources of water and where food is plentiful.

◁ *As pet birds, cockatiels are underrated, but those who keep them are very familiar with their endearing ways.*

⇧ **The crow-sized yellow-tailed black cockatoo** is one of the cockatiel's closest relatives. It is only found in Australia and Tasmania.

How they live in the wild

Cockatiels, like most parrot-like birds, are highly social creatures. In the wild, most male and female cockatiels live as paired-up birds within their flock. The size of the flock can vary from a few dozen individuals to several hundred, or sometimes over a thousand, birds. The main food of wild cockatiels are the seeds of acacia trees, grasses, and agricultural crops, particularly wheat. They will feed both on the ground and in trees, and where food is plentiful they congregate in large flocks. In northern Australia, cockatiels are nomadic and they roam in search of good feeding sites and suitable nesting holes throughout the year. In southern Australia they are migratory birds and breed seasonally, timing breeding with periods when food is abundant.

A wild bird's typical day

Cockatiels are well-known to be light sleepers and they are easily disturbed at night when they will take flight if something frightens them. Normally they will be awake before sunrise and become active as they prepare to fly to their first feeding grounds. Cockatiels fly fast, at about 35-40mph (56-64kph), so they can cover many miles in a few minutes. This gives them the opportunity to exploit food sources over a large territory each day. After rousing, the flock will make its way to the first feeding grounds, typically in acacia trees or fields of wheat. The flock is quite noisy as they take off; their calls keep paired birds in contact with each other and warn the flock of any dangers. Cockatiels are vulnerable to attacks from hawks, so they have to be alert at all times.

The birds soon arrive at their feeding grounds and will stay here for some time until they have filled their crops. They will then spend some time resting and playing together in any nearby trees. They feed intermittently throughout the day and may travel to several different feeding sites. Since their food is generally dry seeds, they need to find water each day, and trips to a river or lake are essential daily activities. Sources of food may be many miles from water, but their swift flight allows them to travel great distances each day if necessary.

⇧ **Like most other species** of parrot, in the wild cockatiels usually nest in holes in trees.

◁ *Paired-up birds* within a flock tend to perch next to one another when they perch.

▷ *Wild cockatiels have to keep* a watch at all time for hawks as they are very vulnerable to sudden attacks.

⇩ *Cockatiels' natural habitat* is dry scrub and open woodland but with a source of water nearby.

A wild bird's typical day

There is usually a period of inactivity around midday. The heat in Australia can be intense around noon so the birds seek shade and remain inactive for an hour or two, just dozing and sleeping intermittently. After this "siesta" they return to feed again at one of their main feeding sites where they will fill up again. They return to their communal roosting site before it begins to get dark.

The daily regime for any breeding birds is different, as they have to incubate eggs and care for their chicks. Cockatiels nest in a hole in a tree and often nest in loose colonies. They lay

⬇ **Both wild birds and pet** cockatiels tend to rest around midday for an hour or two.

◁ **The pair bond between breeding** birds is very strong and they will frequently preen each other.

The males sing ⬄ **loudly** at the females, almost shouting at them in their excitement, prior to mating; their behavior is not very subtle!

between two and seven eggs, five being the usual number. The male and female share the tasks of incubation and feeding of the young. As with other parrots, the chicks are fed regurgitated food which has been partially digested by the parents. Usually the female stays at the nest for most of the day, while the male searches for food and returns to feed the chicks. At night, the male may take over incubation or brooding. Life for the breeding birds is therefore much harder as they have to travel further each day between the nest hole and feeding and drinking sites. However, birds will join their flock wherever possible, at least for part of the day.

Chicks develop rapidly

The eggs hatch after about 19-21 days' incubation and the chicks leave the nest (fledge) by the time they are about four weeks old. However, the young birds are still dependent on their parents, mainly

◁ *These chicks are a few days old, but will be able to fly within a few weeks when they will leave their nest.*

◁ *After leaving the nest, the young remain dependent on their parents for food and protection for several weeks.*

the male, for being fed and the "weaning" process may take several more weeks. During this time, the young birds learn how to feed and they join up with their flock and gradually become independent of their parents. If the birds' food supply remains plentiful, the parents will start to rear a new clutch of eggs, often before their first brood have become fully independent.

Cockatiels can breed before they are a year old. Mortality of the young birds is high during the first few weeks of life and most young birds do not survive to breeding age. Many fall prey to hawks or other predators, or disease, or fail to find enough food. Only the fittest birds survive to find a mate and breed.

chapter 2

The cockatiel as a companion

Unlike some parrot-like birds, cockatiels have adapted well to life in captivity. Since their main food is dry seed, and they come from a rather dry environment, they can live well in our homes provided they are given good accommodation and plenty of time with other birds or their keepers. Although they can occasionally make fairly loud sounds, they rarely cause any problems with repeated loud noises. Their natural repertoire of calls comprises some sharp whistling contact calls, and the males have a cheerful, rambling, whistling song. Some pet birds do learn to imitate human speech as well, and the males usually mimic human speech more commonly than the females.

Underrated as pet birds

They are usually quite active birds with a friendly, inquisitive nature. They can be kept as pairs or as a flock in an aviary. Where a bird is kept on its own as a pet, it will need plenty of time out of the cage in the company of its substitute flock of humans. Being highly social birds, they are not aggressive by nature. They have an easy-going approach to life, while also being intelligent birds. Indeed cockatiels are underrated as companion birds

Cockatiels are not particularly loud birds.

⇧ **Cockatiels have a repertoire** *of whistles and piping notes which are not likely to cause anyone a noise problem.*

bird

and tend to make much better housemates than many other types of parrot.

The behavior of a cockatiel as an adult will vary depending on the methods by which it was raised. Birds which have been raised mainly by their natural parents make the best pets. They may not be as tame and confiding as immature birds who have been hand reared, but as adults, parent-raised birds behave more normally. They have more self-confidence and indeed are more self-reliant. Hand-reared birds tend to be very dependent on constant human company for the rest of their lives and are more vulnerable to behavioral problems as adults. Many other parrot-like birds are very nervous of new situations, or unfamiliar people, or sudden changes in their living conditions but cockatiels, perhaps because they are a nomadic species, adapt well to changes that would upset other birds.

⇧ ⇨ *It is best to avoid allowing the bird on your shoulder (faces may be bitten), and children should be supervised when handling a bird.*

Long-lived birds
Despite their small size, cockatiels can live well into their teens and even into their twenties when given good quality care. As active birds, they do need plenty of opportunity each day to be able to fly. Like other parrots, they can be taught to accept several requests or commands from their keepers, including flight requests; generally cockatiels learn fast with reward-based training techniques (see pages 50-1).

⇧ *While cockatiels are often hand reared, birds raised by their natural parents make better pets and are likely to experience fewer behavioral problems when they grow up to be adults.*

Cockatiels as aviary birds

Many people keep cockatiels outdoors as aviary birds. Since these birds are generally very sociable they are often kept as a flock of birds, and they can even be kept with smaller birds, such as small finches and canaries in a mixed aviary in a garden. Cockatiels are not aggressive birds so provided the aviary is large enough for the number of birds kept, there should be no problems housing the birds in this way. There should also be plenty of places the birds can perch and climb around to prevent them squabbling over favored perches.

Minor squabbles ⇨ sometimes occur between birds, but these rarely turn serious.

⇧*Cockatiels are commonly kept outdoors as aviary birds.*

Breeding in the aviary
Cockatiels will breed readily and provided there are plenty of choices of nesting boxes they will breed freely in a colony aviary with little aggression between the birds. They usually lay four or five eggs per clutch and can have several clutches each year. Since they do breed so easily, you can quickly end up with far too many birds for the size of your aviary, so breeding may need to be limited to prevent overcrowding. A good-sized aviary housing several birds certainly allows the birds to live more natural lives and cockatiels are quite active birds compared to some other parrot-like species. When starting to keep these birds in an aviary, you might begin with just two or three pairs. So, an aviary for this number of birds would need to be about 12ft (3.6m) long by 6ft (1.8m) wide and 6ft (1.8m) high. The birds need to be protected

Aviary birds are usually active and happy

A well-designed garden aviary with cockatiels is an attractive feature which allows birds to socialize with each other and interact in more natural ways than can be provided for a bird housed indoors in a cage. Male cockatiels have an attractive warbling song, and this adds to their appeal. Again, unlike some other parrot-like birds, cockatiels are not likely to cause serious noise-nuisance problems for your neighbors when kept outdoors.

⇧ *A naturalistic aviary* with plenty of perching space provides good stimulation for the birds. **The birds will investigate** any holes that ⇨ may appear to be suitable for nesting.

from the extremes of weather including cold frosty nights, so they will need a wind- and rain-proof shelter attached to the aviary as well. (See pages 44-5 for more details of aviary construction.)

Cockatiel color mutations

Since cockatiels have been bred in captivity for over a hundred years, a great number of color varieties or mutations have been bred. As with the breeding of any mutations in captivity, much of this is done by forced pairing of closely related birds who are of a similar colour, or at least carry the genes for the desired color. So, daughters may be paired with their fathers, brothers with sisters, etc. In the wild, post-fledging behaviors operate to prevent such inbreeding, and birds tend to mate with unrelated flock peers.

Breeding for specific colors
The result of the process of artificial selection (forced pairings) in captivity is that birds can be produced in a range of predictable colors. However, the problem with this is that the strength of the birds' constitution is compromised by such unnatural inbreeding. Inbred birds may have shortened life expectancy, be

◁ **This mutation is** *a pastelface cinnamon pearl pied cockatiel.*

⬇ **Two pied cockatiels** *engage in a session of mutual preening.*

⇧ **Lutino birds** *are white with some yellow.*

⇨ **It's difficult to tell** *the sex of some birds due to the color mutation.*

⇧ **This male cockatiel** *shows the normal 'wild-type' gray colouring.*

more vulnerable to ailments or have their senses impaired. For example, lutino and albino (yellow and white) birds are not able to see the world in color, as they lack pigmentation in their eyes. The wild type or normal gray cockatiel has come about after many millions of years of evolution and natural selection in the birds' natural habitat. Most wild birds which deviate from the normal coloration fail to survive to breed as they succumb to predation or other adverse environmental effects during their first few months of life.

Cockatiel color mutations

There are dozens of color mutations and the following is just a short sample of the more common varieties.

Pearl

Pearl birds have a fine white and colored lace patterning over much of their plumage. Cinnamon pearls have this laced pattern in a warm brown. Gray pearls have it in gray, etc. Males may lose this pattern at the first molt.

Lutino

Lutino birds are white with some pale yellow in the plumage. They have pale or pink feet and red eyes but retain the orange-red ear patch.

Pieds

These are mainly white birds with some even patches of black in the plumage. Pieds with plain white faces are perceived to be superior examples of this mutation.

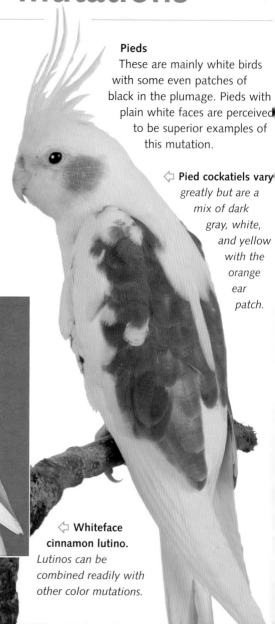

⇦ **Pied cockatiels vary** *greatly but are a mix of dark gray, white, and yellow with the orange ear patch.*

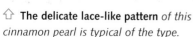

⇧ **The delicate lace-like pattern** *of this cinnamon pearl is typical of the type.*

⇦ **Whiteface cinnamon lutino.** *Lutinos can be combined readily with other color mutations.*

Cinnamon
These birds lack the dark melanin pigment, so the normal gray is replaced with a warm brown color.

Albino
These birds lack all pigmentation, being plain white. They have red eyes with poor vision. The feet are pink and the bill a pale horn color.

Whiteface
This mutation is uniform pale gray over much of the body, but the head lacks all pigmentation, being plain white.

⇧ **Cinnamon male.** *This has a the same pattern as a normal bird, but the gray areas are a warm brown.*

⬂ **Lutino (left) and albino.** *The albino is plain white with red eyes and a pale beak.*

⇦ **Whiteface pastel silver.** *This has the facial plumage in a very diluted, pale form. The whiteface cockatiel can be combined with most other color mutations as well as feather patterns.*

⇧ **Whiteface male.** *The male has a darker gray body than the female and a white face, neck, and wing bars.*

CHAPTER 3

Where to look for a bird

There are many different places where you can obtain a cockatiel. While pet shops and some garden centers might seem the most obvious sources, you can also check ads in birdkeeping magazines, such as *Parrots* magazine. Breeders and those selling older birds often advertise birds for sale in local papers as well. While birds are also advertised on the internet, you should make sure you visit the bird in its current home and that you trust the seller before acquiring the bird. Also make sure you have some form of guarantee as to the bird's health before parting with your money and get a detailed receipt for your bird which includes the date of purchase and the seller's name. Parent-reared birds tend to make better pets than hand-reared ones as they are less likely to over-bond to one person when they become adult. Also, they are more self-reliant as adults than hand-reared birds.

Since cockatiels breed so freely there are actually far more of these birds in need of good homes than there are good homes available for them. Cockatiels often end up in rescue centres and sanctuaries. Some of these places foster

◁ ***Apart from budgies,*** *cockatiels are the most common parrot-like birds to be sold in pet shops.*

their birds out to suitable homes so you may be able to give a bird a good home without having to obtain one from a shop or breeder. In this situation, you will be adopting, rather than owning the bird. Cockatiels are adaptable birds. While some so-called second-hand birds may come with a history of behavioral problems, this is not likely to be the case with cockatiels. Also, if an older bird has always been a pet bird (rather than an outdoor aviary bird), you may be able to offer it better one-to-one attention than staff at a sanctuary are able to provide. To find details of these sources you can

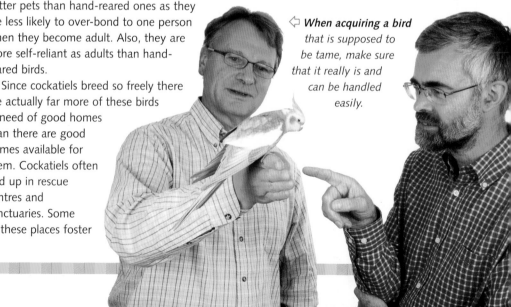

◁ ***When acquiring a bird*** *that is supposed to be tame, make sure that it really is and can be handled easily.*

Acquiring a bird

⇧ **Take care when using** the internet to buy a bird and always see it in its home before purchase.

Rescue centers may ⇨ **sometimes** foster cockatiels out to a good home.

search the internet using the words "parrot sanctuary" or "parrot rescue" or "parrot re-homing," etc. Or you could contact the ASPCA and ask them for details of bona fide sources of birds in need of good homes.

If a bird is advertised as tame, make sure that you see that the bird really is comfortable with being handled, at least by the seller. In the world of birdkeeping, it is a case of "let the buyer beware," so take your time when selecting a bird from the range of sources available.

What to look for in a healthy

Most birds have a behavioral adaptation to try to hide any signs of being unwell and endeavor to appear normal at all times. They can do this right up to the time they are seriously ill, so you need to be able to recognize a healthy bird by looking for the usual signs of good health.

Healthy birds are generally quite active for most of the day. The eyes should be bright and wide open. There should be no discharge from the nostrils and the breathing should be silent. The bird should be alert and well aware of things going on around it. The body feathers should be in good condition. They should not be fluffed up but slightly smoothed down. The bird should be eating normally and passing droppings normally, without undue straining. The area around the vent should be clean, not soiled by droppings. When at rest or sleeping a healthy bird usually stands on one foot.

Look for a healthy, alert bird

Birds that are unwell will show the opposite of these signs: fluffed up feathers, inattentive, sleepy, with dull, perhaps half-closed, eyes. Where you see a bird which does not show the normal healthy signs, something may be wrong, so take care if you are considering buying such a bird. You can always ask the owner to have the bird checked by a specialist avian vet before you buy it and see the vet's report. Failing this, it is certainly worth having any newly acquired bird checked by an avian vet within a day or two of acquiring it.

This bird is attentive ⇨ *and well aware of things going on around him.*

Bird alert

No discharge from nostrils

Eyes bright

Breathing silent

Body feathers in good condition

Vent area clean

Check the feather condition as this reflects the bird's state of health.

⇦ **Soiled and damaged feathers** can indicate a poor state of health.

Hand-reared birds may ⇨ over-bond to one person when they grow up. It can pay to acquire an older bird as its character will be more fully formed.

⇩ **The lowered head** is submissive as this bird asks for its head to be caressed.

Older birds can make good pets

Some birds that are sold as immature and "cuddly tame," usually from a pet shop, do not reveal their true character until they become adult. Immature birds, particularly hand-reared ones, tend to show submissive behaviors to anyone. So, there is an advantage in getting an older bird (generally from a private sale) in that the bird's true character will be well formed and there are unlikely to be any major changes to this. Older cockatiels are often sold for genuine reasons. While these birds do not suffer from behavioral problems as commonly as many other parrots, these do sometimes occur. Such problems can include nervousness and self-plucking, so check carefully with the bird's current owner before agreeing to take it on. Often behavioral problems are not so difficult to address and remedy, as is discussed later in Chapter 10.

CHAPTER 4

Using their senses: sight

A cockatiel's keenest sense is vision and these birds have a number of adaptations to their eyes which gives them better eyesight than humans. The part of the eye that you can see is only a small part of the eyeball itself, which is much larger. The skull of a bird and its eye sockets reveal the true size of the eyes. Being placed on the sides of their head, the bird's eyes give them almost 360 degree 'all-round' vision, both vertically and horizontally. This ensures they can easily spot any danger

⇩ *The cockatiel's near all-round field of vision helps to warn it of danger from all directions.*

which may come from any direction. They also have good binocular (stereo) vision as we do, for objects which are near and in front of them. All parrots can switch back and forth between their all-round monocular vision to close-up stereo vision in a split second.

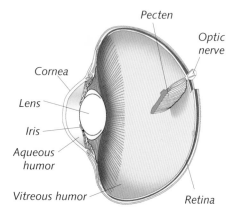

⇧ *The cockatiel's eye is similar to ours but the vascular pecten is unique to birds. It is thought to help improve blood flow to the retina.*

Cockatiels see more colors than we do
Cockatiels' eyes are somewhat flattened, not spherical like ours, and they have limited eye-movement within the socket, so they tend to move the whole head when examining objects. Like other birds, they also have a third eyelid which blinks diagonally across the eye. This keeps the surface of the eye clean. While human color vision is limited to mixes of red, green and blue light, most birds see ultraviolet light as another one or two

Cockatiel biology

⇨ *Cockatiels have very flexible* necks. Movement here overcomes the limited movement of the eyes within their sockets.

⇩ *In addition to their two eyelids,* cockatiels have a third membrane that blinks diagonally across the eye.

High speed vision

Birds process visual information at a much higher rate than we do. Our brain takes in about 16 images per second through our eyes. Films and videos are projected at around 25 frames per second, so this gives humans the illusion of a moving image. But birds process over 70 images per second, so a normal TV

⇧ *As well as having superior* color vision, birds process more images per second than humans. This may be an adaptation necessary for high-speed flying.

distinct colors as well. This is thought to help them distinguish between the sexes, as some color differences between males and females may only be visible in UV colors. Such vision may also help them identify some foods they commonly eat from a distance and to determine which of these are ripe.

screen does not appear as a moving image to a bird. Since cockatiels fly at around 40mph (64kph), this adaptation ensures they can process information at the speed needed for a fast-moving bird in flight.

Hearing, touch, temperature, an

Birds do not have an external ear, but the opening to the ears lies just below and behind the eyes. In cockatiels it is under the red feathers. The feathers covering the ear are sparse and allow sound waves to pass through easily. A cockatiel's ears work in much the same way as ours. Vibrations of air caused by sound pass down the open ear tube to the eardrum. Here, these vibrations are passed through a tiny bone

A touch-sensitive warning system
The whole of a bird's body is sensitive to touch through the skin. This includes disturbance to feathers, light touching,

⇨ *The three semi-circular canals are used to detect gravity in the three-dimensional world in which birds live.*

Fluid-filled semi-circular canals

⟁ *If you look closely, you can see that the ear-covert feathers are sparser than the other head feathers.*

Middle ear

Inner ear

to the inner fluid-filled ear, which relays nervous (electrical) signals to the brain. Cockatiels hear a similar range of sounds to humans; and certainly produce sounds in a similar range. In addition to processing sound, the inner ear contains a series of semi-circular canals, again like our own. These are used to detect the force of gravity and to maintain balance which in turn ensures that the bird can keep an appropriate body position, particularly when flying. Despite the banking, diving, and rolling movements birds use in flight, they tend to keep their heads as level as possible at all times while flying.

Position of ear

spicy foods, such as peppers. Most of their taste buds are not on the tongue but the roof of the mouth so the tongue transfers minute food samples here to be tested before eating.

A parrot's feet are very sensitive to touch, particularly vibrations. This allows them be aware of anything which might be crawling along their branch or perch at night when vision is very limited. The bird is aware of which side of their branch the disturbance comes from and

⇧ **The tongue is used** to test new surfaces not just for taste, but for texture and temperature.

and pain. Two areas are particularly sensitive to touch for parrots: the tongue and the feet. Parrots are perhaps unique among birds in the way they use their tongues. The first contact with some new food or object is usually with the front of the beak that is used to prod it, perhaps to see if it is safe. Then the tongue is used much like a fingertip to feel it. A cockatiel's tongue is very muscular as well as sensitive to temperature and texture and is used to find the weakest point in nuts and seeds before cracking them open. Parrots experience a similar range of tastes to us – sweet, sour, bitter, and salty. But they cannot taste hot

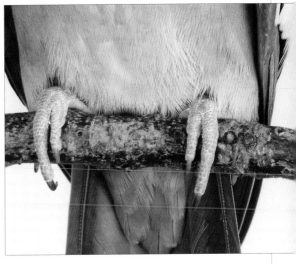

⇧ **The bird's feet can detect** even slight vibrations which may pass along its perch, and cockatiels are particularly sensitive to disturbance at night.

can take evasive action if needed. Indeed, cockatiels are very sensitive to nighttime disturbance. As with other parrots, cockatiels seem to have a poor sense of smell.

Breathing and blood circulation

Oxygen in fresh air is used to "burn" the bird's fuel, which is the food that is broken down in the bird's gut to supply the nutrients that are circulating in its bloodstream. This fuel is used for bodily functions, such as keeping warm, and of course for powering the muscles required by the bird's range of activities including flight. Flight is extremely demanding in terms of energy use. As a result, birds have evolved an elaborate breathing system which ensures oxygen is taken up at the elevated rates needed to support such levels of activity. The waste products of this activity are mainly carbon dioxide and water, and these are eliminated as the bird exhales with the same speed at which oxygen is used. Breathing is very rapid while the bird is flying.

Air sacs for efficient breathing
In terms of effort, the difference between a bird walking and then flying is a bit like the difference between a car trundling around in first gear and then being driven at high speed in top gear. In addition to their lungs, which are similar to ours, birds have a system of air-sacs throughout their bodies. By shunting air around these air-sacs at high speed, birds can deliver a constant supply of fresh air to the lungs. In this system the air travels over the lungs in the same direction all

⇧ *Cockatiels are buoyant, agile flyers and can move at considerable speed.*

⇩ *Unlike flying, walking uses relatively little energy.*

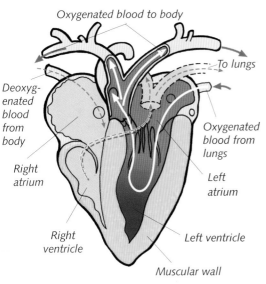

Oxygenated blood to body

To lungs

Deoxygenated blood from body

Oxygenated blood from lungs

Right atrium

Left atrium

Right ventricle

Left ventricle

Muscular wall

⇧ **A parrot's heart** is very similar to ours, but it works at a much higher rate. This allows for sustained flight at considerable speed.

blood temperature is 104-106°F (40-41°C), while the human's is only 98.6°F (37°C). All these adaptations allow a parrot's body to operate at a much higher rate than is found in almost any mammal. This is needed to ensure that the birds can carry out sustained flight without becoming exhausted.

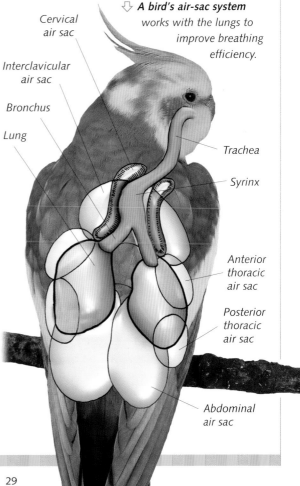

⇩ **A bird's air-sac system** works with the lungs to improve breathing efficiency.

Cervical air sac

Interclavicular air sac

Bronchus

Lung

Trachea

Syrinx

Anterior thoracic air sac

Posterior thoracic air sac

Abdominal air sac

the time, rather than just being sucked in and blown out as with our breathing. These refinements mean a bird's breathing abilities are more efficient than ours.

All birds have a four-chambered heart similar to ours and the bird's blood circulation system works at a high-speed level to match its high-speed breathing requirements. Even while at rest, a cockatiel's heart beats at about 140 times per minute – more than twice the rate of a human heart. When flying, this increases to around 900 beats per minute and this is quite normal for small birds. A cockatiel's normal

The digestive system

Cockatiels concentrate on finding seeds as their main food source, and most of these are seeds of cereals and grasses. These are high in complex carbohydrates and are not digested as rapidly as sweet foods, such as fruits. Some other seeds and most nuts are high in fat, and the birds will show a preference for these high value foods when they can find them.

⇧ **Cockatiels can eat** a range of tiny seeds that many larger birds would find difficult to de-husk.

⇧ **Young birds have to learn** how to develop beak skills and will play with inedible objects to this end.

Despite the bird's small size, its beak is a powerful, universal tool with sharp cutting edges which can be used with great skill. The beak is used in combination with the sensitive and muscular tongue to examine and manipulate items of food. Unlike most other birds, parrots use their beak in a chewing action to chop up their food into small pieces before swallowing. They also discard parts of the food which are poor in nutrients, such as the husks around the seeds, by using the beak to peel this off. The food then passes into the bird's crop.

High-speed digestion

The crop is an extension of the esophagus, the tube which connects the mouth to the true stomach, where food is stored before the next stages of digestion can take place. It then passes to the proventriculus, a part of the bird's stomach where proper digestion begins as digestive juices are secreted and mixed with the food. Next the food passes to the gizzard. This is a muscular part of the stomach where food is ground down under great pressure from the grinding action of this part of the gut. The inner

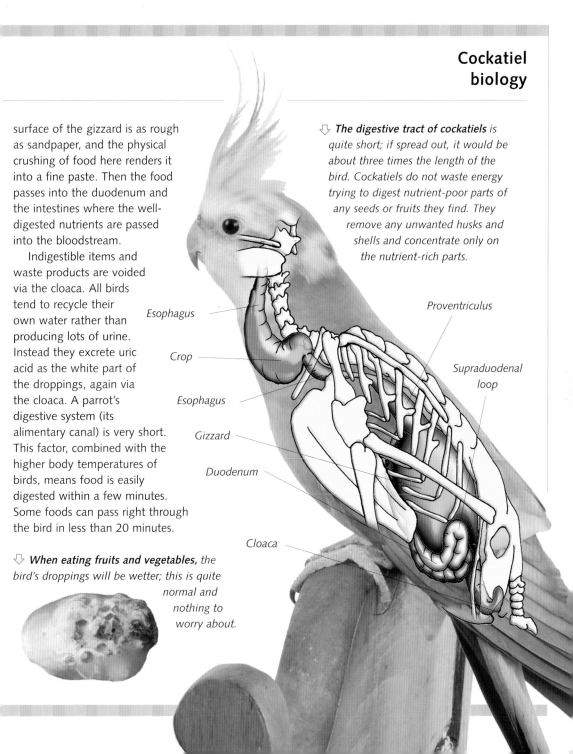

surface of the gizzard is as rough as sandpaper, and the physical crushing of food here renders it into a fine paste. Then the food passes into the duodenum and the intestines where the well-digested nutrients are passed into the bloodstream.

Indigestible items and waste products are voided via the cloaca. All birds tend to recycle their own water rather than producing lots of urine. Instead they excrete uric acid as the white part of the droppings, again via the cloaca. A parrot's digestive system (its alimentary canal) is very short. This factor, combined with the higher body temperatures of birds, means food is easily digested within a few minutes. Some foods can pass right through the bird in less than 20 minutes.

⇩ *The digestive tract of cockatiels is quite short; if spread out, it would be about three times the length of the bird. Cockatiels do not waste energy trying to digest nutrient-poor parts of any seeds or fruits they find. They remove any unwanted husks and shells and concentrate only on the nutrient-rich parts.*

⇩ **When eating fruits and vegetables,** the bird's droppings will be wetter; this is quite normal and nothing to worry about.

Esophagus

Crop

Esophagus

Gizzard

Duodenum

Cloaca

Proventriculus

Supraduodenal loop

CHAPTER 5

How cockatiels fly

ockatiels are essentially flying creatures which have evolved over millions of years to perfect their flying abilities. Flying for these birds is as natural as walking is for us. To keep weight to a minimum, birds never carry any excess baggage so they do not normally carry large fat deposits and practically every cell in their body is modified to reduce weight. They have very light hollow bones and very light feathers. They also have a powerful "engine": the massive pectoral muscles and large heart which allow fast sustained flight.

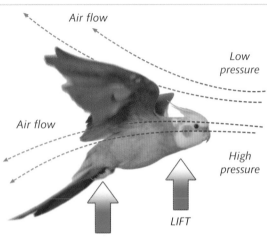

⇧ **The aerofoil shape of a bird's wing** is similar to that employed on an aircraft. When air flows rapidly over this curved surface, lift is generated. To generate this air flow, aircraft use engines while birds flap their wings (with the outer primary feathers doing most of the work).

⇧ **The barbs of each feather** fan out like leaf veins. Each is connected to the next one by a series of Velcro-like hooks and loops.

The vertical cross-section of a bird's wing has a slight curve and it is this simple shape which results in birds being able to generate lift. As air flows over the upper surface of the wing, it accelerates which causes a drop in pressure relative to that of the air passing under the wings. This results in the wings (and therefore the bird!) being pushed upwards. The faster the air flows over the wing, the greater the amount of lift. The outer half of the bird's wing, the ten primary feathers, provide the propulsion needed to ensure this airflow is maintained. As the bird flaps downwards and backwards, air is pushed backwards over the wings. In addition to gravity, the main limiting factor in flight is the braking action caused by friction between the bird and the air, called drag. However, the bird's streamlined shape minimizes drag.

Cockatiels in flight

Skilled aerobatic flyers

There are several forms of flight. In powered flight, the wings beat regularly and the bird is able to climb easily and rapidly in the air. Cockatiels fly at about 40mph (64kph) and can cover huge distances when airborne for only a few minutes. This form of flapping flight is expensive in terms of energy use, but the bird's whole body is very well adapted to the needs of flight. The direction of the

⇩ *Landing requires fine-tuned skills and precision technique which are acquired through trial and error. Sometimes the bird makes a minor mistake, as here. The bird has misjudged the perch and stalled slightly too early. He corrects himself by flapping until he regains the perch.*

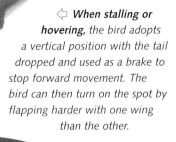

⇦ *When stalling or hovering, the bird adopts a vertical position with the tail dropped and used as a brake to stop forward movement. The bird can then turn on the spot by flapping harder with one wing than the other.*

Hovering skills take time to learn.

wind relative to the bird's direction greatly affects flying speed. When flying against the wind the bird will travel slower, but cockatiels can do over 50mph (80kph) in a favorable wind.

When coming in to land, cockatiels hold their wings angled downwards and glide without flapping. Since gliding is passive, it results in a loss of height as the bird moves forward, but on landing the bird deliberately stalls just before it makes contact with the perch and grasps this with its feet. Cockatiels are very aerobatic birds; they can hover, turn 360 degrees without flying forward, and change direction rapidly whenever needed. The whole of the bird's body and wings are used for each flying task. While the primaries are used in propulsion, they are also used as air-brakes when employing a reverse-thrust action on landing. Good flying skills for a wild bird ensure its survival. Companion birds usually retain these abilities provided they are given the space and opportunities for regular safe flying sessions while living in the home.

The large tail permits rapid change of direction during flight.

Learning to fly

Cockatiels leave the nest (fledge) when they are about four weeks old. But they remain highly dependent on their parents for their food and safety for several more weeks. On first leaving the nest, the fledglings make their first attempts to fly. While the urge to fly is very strong in the baby birds, at this age their *abilities* to fly are rather poor. This is because the skills of flying have to be learned by each bird through simple trial and error experiences. Young birds may practice flapping while perched. This helps to strengthen their pectoral muscles (the main muscles used to fly) and gives them the feel of the power of their wings and the lift this generates.

This stance shows the bird is about to fly.

⬇ **Note the splayed wings,** *body feathers held down tightly, staring eyes and the alert pose with the head held up.*

Flying skills are soon acquired

Soon they gain the confidence to take off for their first flight but often they crash-land clumsily. However, after a few attempts at flight their abilities to manoeuvre and control their

◁ **This bird's body language** *says it all. He's ready for take-off!*

speed and direction while airborne begin to improve and they soon land with more precision. So, it is vital to encourage these youngsters to fly at this stage. This ensures that the birds develop normally and that their muscles, including their heart, also develop as they should do. If such young birds are denied the opportunities to learn to fly, they often fail ever to learn to fly properly for the rest of their lives. This in itself can cause the birds to exhibit behavioral problems as they are unable to

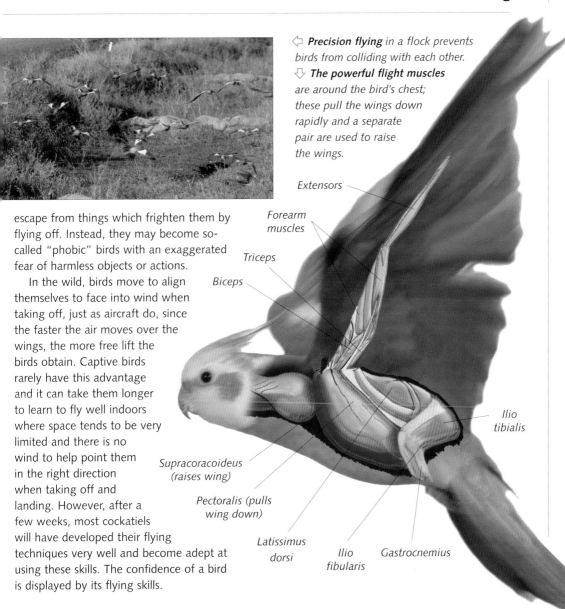

⬅ **Precision flying** in a flock prevents birds from colliding with each other.
⬇ **The powerful flight muscles** are around the bird's chest; these pull the wings down rapidly and a separate pair are used to raise the wings.

Extensors

Forearm muscles

Triceps

Biceps

Ilio tibialis

Supracoracoideus (raises wing)

Pectoralis (pulls wing down)

Latissimus dorsi

Ilio fibularis

Gastrocnemius

escape from things which frighten them by flying off. Instead, they may become so-called "phobic" birds with an exaggerated fear of harmless objects or actions.

In the wild, birds move to align themselves to face into wind when taking off, just as aircraft do, since the faster the air moves over the wings, the more free lift the birds obtain. Captive birds rarely have this advantage and it can take them longer to learn to fly well indoors where space tends to be very limited and there is no wind to help point them in the right direction when taking off and landing. However, after a few weeks, most cockatiels will have developed their flying techniques very well and become adept at using these skills. The confidence of a bird is displayed by its flying skills.

Safety in the home

The main factors to bear in mind regarding the safety of your bird are avoiding obvious household dangers and having your bird trained to accept some flight requests from you.

Windows and external doors should be kept closed before you ask your bird to come out of its cage.

⇧ **Small birds and cats** do not mix! For the safety of the bird, keep them apart at all times.

Alternatively, you can cover windows with a suitable mesh which allows them to be open while preventing the bird from escaping. Rooms where your bird is allowed to fly should have any large windows covered with net curtains to prevent the bird thinking it can fly through the glass. Large mirrors are very confusing for birds, so these should be removed, covered, or reversed. Ceiling fans can cause a fearful reaction in some birds as the blades (even when not switched on) may be seen as a predator's wings, so it's best that these fans are not present in the same room in which a bird is kept or allowed to fly. The kitchen presents many dangers to birds; these include hot surfaces, ovens, and electrical appliances, so it's

⇧ ⇨ **Birds may find** their reflection intriguing but when they are in flight, large mirrors are very confusing to them. Remove them from the room.

⇧ *A small piece of biscuit is this bird's favorite treat. This is shown to him as a reward when asking him to go down to a new place for the first time.*

best to avoid having birds here. Birds may also drown if they fall into a toilet or any other container holding water.

A careful introduction to any new room

When a bird is being encouraged to use an unfamiliar room and is allowed to fly there, it will need to be introduced to the room carefully. Without this introduction to a room, the bird will not know which places are safe and suitable to land on. This introduction stage is a fairly formal training process where the bird is asked to step down onto those places to which you would like him to go and is then given a reward, perhaps a food treat, for doing so. Suitable places could include chair backs, the sofa, window ledges, table tops, and a

stand for the bird (see page 45). After the bird has been introduced to these places as perches, when he does fly, he will be more confident about where to land and therefore much less likely to crash land.

If your bird is ever suddenly frightened of something and takes flight and crash lands, do *not* approach him until a few moments have passed and he has collected his senses. If you approach a frightened bird too readily, he will associate you with the fearful incident and may become very afraid of you.

⇩ *Don't approach a crash-landed bird immediately. Wait a while until he has recovered his senses.*

CHAPTER 6

Choosing the right cage

The amount of time your bird spends in a cage each day will have a great effect on its quality of life and behavior. Cockatiels kept as companion or pet birds should be encouraged to spend many hours each day out of their cage so that they can interact

◁ *A small cage is not suitable for active birds such as cockatiels; make sure your bird has ample space to encourage activity.*

with people and/or other birds. This is essential for their well-being.

The cage should be large enough so that the bird can easily flap its wings while it is inside. So, the main factor in deciding on the minimum cage size is the bird's wingspan – this is the measurement from wing-tip to wing-tip of the bird's wings when they are fully outstretched, as though the bird were in flight. Cockatiels

⇨ *The length from the center of the bird's back to the end of its outstretched wing is 10 inches; so the full wingspan is 20 inches.*

have a wingspan of around 20in (50cm). So a cage where all three measurements (the height, depth, and width) exceed the bird's wingspan will at least allow the bird to flap its wings, provided there are no other obstructions, such as too many toys within the cage. However, the cage should also allow the bird to fly while inside it. Therefore, a better guide is to ensure the length of the cage is more than twice the bird's wingspan. So a suitable **minimum** cage size would be 21in (53cm) high, 21in (53cm) deep and 42in (106cm) long.

Check the cage's bar spacing
While the best and most expensive cages are made of stainless steel, most are made of mild steel which is then coated with various layers of paint. The paintwork is usually stove enamelled. This process hardens the paint and ensures it cannot be damaged or picked off by the bird.

⇨ *Cockatiels will use a good cage as a climbing frame. This is best achieved by having more horizontal bars than vertical ones.*

get its head between the bars. Therefore, the spacing between the bars should be less than ¾in (2cm). It is an advantage to choose a cage with the food bowls mounted on swing-feeders which allows the food to be changed from outside the cage.

⇩ *Food bowls which can be changed from outside the cage make it easier for others to care for your bird if you go away for a few days.*

⇧ *This is a well-made cage of sound design and construction.*

The bars should be sufficiently thick and strong enough so that the bird cannot bend or damage them. Damaged bars can result in the protective coating being removed by the bird. Cockatiels enjoy being able to climb, and this allows them some exercise. To aid this, the cage should have horizontal, rather than just vertical, bars. For the bird's safety, it is important that the bird cannot

Setting up the cage

Since most cages are made with wire on all sides, without a solid side, the cage should be positioned with its back against a wall. This will give the bird a greater feeling of security.

the cage. If the bird is nervous, the height of the top perch should be increased, so that the bird can look down on you. If the cage has a grill just above its floor tray, this should be removed. Cockatiels are ground feeders and enjoy having access to the floor. The cage floor should be covered with newspaper sheets that are changed each day.

Choose perches of varying thickness
To ensure the bird's feet are exercised properly, there should be a variety of perches in the cage and these should be provided in a range of different thicknesses. Usually, perches supplied with a new cage are of uniform and often excessive thickness. As with other birds, cockatiels have a locking mechanism in their feet when perched which allows them to grip the perch with little effort, but this does not work on thick perches. For

⇧ *The cage should be placed in a well-lit area, near, but not too close, to a window. The back of the cage should be set against a solid wall.*

If possible, position the cage so the bird can see out of a window, perhaps onto your garden where the comings and goings of other birds will add some interest, but make sure the cage is never in full sun as this can very easily cause overheating. The cage should be high enough so that the top perches allow the bird to be at your eye level when you are standing next to

your bird to perch comfortably, most perches should have a diameter which varies

⇨ *This natural wood perch is quite thin and has the bark left on it. The bird can wrap its toes right around the perch.*

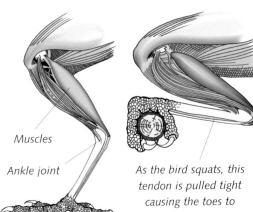

Muscles

Ankle joint

As the bird squats, this tendon is pulled tight causing the toes to grip the perch.

⇧ **When standing,** a bird uses more energy in its leg muscles. If a perch is too thick, the bird is forced to stand and cannot grip the perch passively.

between ⅜in (1cm) to ¾in (2cm). This allows the bird to grip the perch properly by wrapping its toes right around the perch. Some other perches can be thicker or even thinner than this.

The benefits of natural wood perches

Perches made from any natural untreated hardwood such as ash, hawthorn, maple, hazel, apple, and cherry are suitable. Rope perches of natural fibers such as cotton, jute, or hemp are also beneficial. Plastic perches should be avoided. Some cockatiels may chew their perches and this helps them exercise their beak. With this in mind perches should be seen as disposable items to be renewed frequently. Since

they get dirty very easily, it is useful to have two sets of perches for each cage so you always have a spare set when needed. Sometimes an abrasive perch is used to keep a bird's claws less sharp. However, cockatiels need fairly sharp claws in order to grip smooth surfaces properly. If you use an abrasive perch, this should be placed low down in the cage and not be the bird's favorite or top perch.

◁ ⇧ **Rope perches stimulate** the bird to exercise. Some have screw ends to attach to the cage bars. Don't use a rope perch as a top or roosting perch. The top perch should be fixed firmly.

Furnishing the cage

The cage should be made as interesting as possible so the way you furnish it is very important to your bird. A great variety of toys are available for parrots now. You should aim to have three or four hanging toys in the cage at a time. But to keep your bird interested and entertained, you should have a collection of hanging toys and change one of these every few days, so the bird does not get bored with having the same ones all the time.

Cockatiels cannot play with foot-held toys like other parrots, but they will happily play with smaller toys on the floor of their cage. These floor toys are often a bird's favorite items to play with, particularly if they can chew them up to destruction. While there are commercially available toys, you can often make or obtain these for little or no cost yourself. Suitable items

⇩ *As befits ground-feeders, cockatiels like to play with small toys on the floor of their cage.*

include small pinecones, small cardboard boxes, clothes pegs, lollipop sticks, pieces of twisted newspaper, small hardwood sticks, and small hard plastic balls. You can also make or purchase puzzle toys. These are used to hold food treats and your bird can be left to work out how to extract them.

⇦ *Toys with parts that rattle or which are made of several movable parts help to keep cockatiels interested and stimulated.*

Toys keep your bird busy

Toys must be safe for your bird so avoid any with small or sharp metal parts that might be detached and swallowed by the bird. Where toys have rings, the rule to bear in mind regarding their safety is that the rings should either be so

If toys have fibers, make sure these are of natural materials.

small that the bird cannot get its head through them, or so large that the bird's whole body can pass easily through. If the bird is aggressive or over-excited when given a mirror, this should be removed; males seem more prone to aggressive behaviors with a mirrors.

You should consider providing your bird with a roosting box in the cage to give him somewhere to hide away and to sleep in. Cockatiels will remain silent when in the box. The box is similar to a nesting box and should be made from half-inch/12mm plywood. The internal measurements should be about 7in (18cm)

⇧ *These hanging toys* are all suitable for cockatiels. There is now a great range of small parrot toys available for these birds.

square by 12in (30cm) high. The box should be placed as high up in the cage as possible and be securely fitted. The entrance hole can be quite large; about 3in (7.5cm) across. Put some wood shavings and perhaps some chewable toys inside to keep the bird occupied when it is in the roosting box.

⇦ *Cockatiels often take to* a roosting box; if it induces a female to lay eggs, it's best removed.

Parrot stands and an aviary

While your bird is out of its cage, there should be several places he can fly to and use. These might include chair backs, window-ledges, tabletops, etc. But your bird should also have at least one stand on which he can play with toys and eat some food while he is out. Stands come in a range of sizes so get one with several different perches which

can also hold food bowls and has plenty of room for fitting toys onto it. In addition to these large stands, you can also get small, portable table-top stands. You can carry these around with you from one room to another. As cockatiels like to use a perch rather than have to stand on a flat surface, these are ideal and most birds will soon use these stands readily.

The benefits of an outdoor flight

Even if you have only one or two cockatiels which are normally kept indoors, it is of great benefit to them if you can give them access to an outdoor aviary to be used during the daytime in good weather. The aviary can be used even in winter on fine mild days. Birds which have access to the outdoors have much better feather condition than indoor birds, so allowing your bird to feel some wind and even some rain on him from time to time will generally improve his feather condition.

Provide protection from direct sun and wind

To encourage flight the aviary should be at least 8ft (2.4m) long; the height should be at least 6ft (1.8m). If you make the back higher, you can have a sloping roof and this allows water to drain off. The aviary should be made from 1in (2.5cm) by ½in (1.25cm) 16 gauge best-quality welded mesh. The 'gauge' is the thickness of the wire. You can use a wooden or metal frame. Where a wooden frame is used, use 2in (5cm) or 3in (7.5cm) square timbers and hang the wire mesh on the *inside* as this gives some protection against the bird chewing the wood. Part of the aviary should be sheltered from rain and direct sun, so use some opaque rigid plastic sheeting for a section of the roof to give some shade.

The aviary floor can be concrete or gravel or left as natural grass. Furnish the aviary with plenty of perches, rope swings, and toys and have swing-feeders fitted as well for your bird's food and water containers.

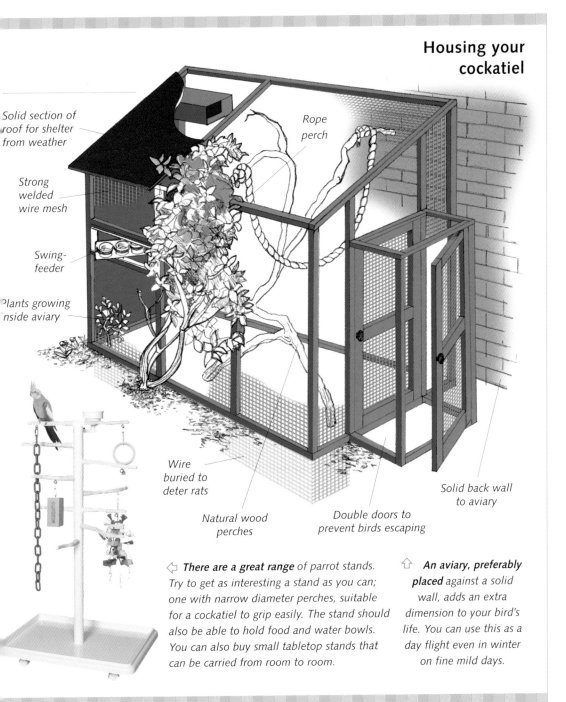

Solid section of roof for shelter from weather

Rope perch

Strong welded wire mesh

Swing-feeder

Plants growing inside aviary

Wire buried to deter rats

Natural wood perches

Double doors to prevent birds escaping

Solid back wall to aviary

⇦ **There are a great range** of parrot stands. Try to get as interesting a stand as you can; one with narrow diameter perches, suitable for a cockatiel to grip easily. The stand should also be able to hold food and water bowls. You can also buy small tabletop stands that can be carried from room to room.

⇧ **An aviary, preferably placed** against a solid wall, adds an extra dimension to your bird's life. You can use this as a day flight even in winter on fine mild days.

CHAPTER 7

What foods are available?

Cockatiels are mainly seed eaters, but they should be given a variety of seeds. This should include millet, canary seed, wheat, oats, and niger seed. The millet can be given as a millet spray. Some cockatiels will also eat

Dry seed mix

Soaked seeds

sunflower and safflower seeds. They should also have access to fresh fruit (apple, grapes), fresh seeding grasses, and some green vegetables, such as groundsel, dandelion, or spinach, on most days. By ensuring

Groundsel

Dandelion leaves

Lettuce

Grapes

Millet   *Apple*

that your bird has a varied diet, this will help to provide him with all the vitamins and minerals needed. The problem of poor diets for captive birds arises because birds are "programmed" to eat foods of the highest energy value which tend to be foods that are high in fat. A *wild* cockatiel needs to eat a lot more food than a captive one, since wild birds have to fly many miles every day in search of food, and they burn off any excess calories. But a pet bird will never be able to exercise at such a rate, so the diet for a captive bird needs to reflect that bird's real food needs.

Composition of foods

Food comprises carbohydrates, fat, and protein; the only other constituents are vitamins, minerals, and water. Grains, fresh fruits, and cereals are high in carbohydrates and these high energy foods are used to keep the bird warm and as a fuel to power the bird's muscles. Nuts and many seeds, such as sunflower seeds, are high in fats. Fat can be stored and broken down and used as fuel later. Legumes (peas and beans) and most cereals (rice, wheat, millet, etc.) are high in protein which is needed to renew and replace body tissues including feathers. For cockatiels the diet should be mainly carbohydrate (about 75-80 percent) with around 15

◁ *Cockatiels appreciate having variety in their diet and this should include leafy green foods.*

Nutritional Values For Some Common Parrot Foods

	Fat	Protein	Carbohydrate
Apple*	0.1%	0.3%	11.5%
Cheese (Cheddar)	34%	25%	0.1%
(Caution: has very high salt content of 1.8%)			
Canary seed	18%	9%	60%
Linseed	64%	12%	22%
Millet*	7%	10%	70%
Pelleted foods*	14%	12%	60%
Legumes/bean mix*	1.4%	21%	45%
Rice*	1.2%	7.3%	77%
Safflower seed*	6%	32%	51%
Sunflower seed	48%	12%	18.6%
Wheat*	2.5%	12%	62%

* indicates the better, low-fat foods.

Note: Lost percentages to 100% are mainly composed of water

percent vegetable protein and only 5-8 percent fat.

In terms of nutrition, it does not matter how these foods are supplied. However, cockatiels have a range of techniques for dealing with the different, more natural foods they may encounter, so a diet based on a variety of seeds and fresh greenstuffs adds interest for the bird. Some human foods are either toxic or can cause your bird to have problems. So do not allow your bird to be given chocolate, coffee, tea, alcohol, or avocado. Salty foods can cause kidney failure, so items such as chips and savoury snacks should never be given to cockatiels.

Unlike many parrots, cockatiels are adapted to a dry seed diet.

⇩ **A seed mix low in fat** is recommended.

The mix should include different cereal and grass seeds, such as canary seed, millet, wheat, rice, and some sunflower, safflower, and linseed.

Feeding your cockatiel

Since the full nutritional needs of a cockatiel cannot be provided for by a dry seed-based diet alone, you'll need to supply other items. By soaking, and preferably sprouting, the seed mixture, this will make the seeds easier to digest and it increases their vitamin content. Legumes (peas and beans) may also be eaten by some cockatiels and it is worth trying your bird on these foods. Legumes cannot be eaten dry, but have to be soaked, and preferably sprouted, to be edible. Legumes are high in protein with little or no fat, so you cannot overfeed a bird on legumes.

Dry legumes

Soaked legumes

⇩ **Some cockatiels like** *like the change of eating soaked seeds and legumes.*

The following diet is recommended for cockatiels

- 60 percent seed mixture comprising millet, canary seed, wheat, oats, niger; you can feed these dry, but offering them soaked and sprouted improves their nutritional content.

- 20 percent fresh greenstuffs and fruit. Try seeding grasses, leafy greens, chickweed, lettuce, apple, pomegranate, grapes.

- 20 percent soaked/sprouted legumes (try mung beans, aduki beans, black-eye beans).

Preparing your bird's food
If you offer a soaked and sprouted seed and legumes diet, you might find it easiest to first mix your seeds (60 percent) and pulses (20 percent) together and store them as a dry mixture. To prepare this, soak one day's amount in water for 12 hours. You can use warm but not hot water, as the heat would kill the mixture and

⇨ **Good quality millet** *can be given as a millet spray. Millet is a good source of some minerals and is low in fat and has good protein content.*

◁ **Green food should be available** *every day. Lettuce, kale, dandelion, and chickweed are all appreciated by most cockatiels and these fresh foods add variety to the birds' diet.*

prevent it sprouting. You'll need about 0.4-0.5oz (12-15 grams) of dry food for each bird. The beans may smell while soaking, but this is quite normal. After 12 hours you can feed the soaked mixture, but it is best to sprout and germinate the mixture following another 12 to 24 hours. Keep the food moist at room temperature (not soaking in water) and rinse it thoroughly several times in cold water to prevent any bacterial contamination. Once tiny white shoots appear, this shows the mixture has germinated and is ready to use. Don't keep this food for more than one day after it is ready to eat, just throw away all leftovers. Don't cook any bean/seed mixes, nor keep them in a fridge. Simply feed it raw.

Vary the bird's diet from time to time to keep him interested in different foods. If your bird is actually eating a varied diet as described, there is little need to supply any other supplements. However, cockatiels kept indoors may be low in vitamin D3 since this is made by the body under direct sunlight (not light through a glass window). This vitamin is used to process calcium in the bird's body. Indoor birds can be given a supplement which contains both vitamin D3 and liquid calcium which you can get from bird food and supplement suppliers.

CHAPTER 8

Understanding behavior

The main reasons for teaching your bird to accept a few training requests from you are much the same as those for training any animal that will be living with you; you'll need to have good communication with your bird if it is to share your home as a companion animal. A trained cockatiel who accepts a few simple requests from you makes a far better companion than a confused, untrained bird who may be nervous of people. Before you make a start on training it is best to understand in more detail the motivations that underlie animal behavior in general.

The behaviors of any animal, including humans, are always carried out for a reason. And the reason is essentially that the animal knows it will derive some benefit from performing the behavior. Birds will drink when thirsty and eat when hungry. They will tidy up their feathers by preening until they feel more comfortable. If something frightens a bird it will try to fly away, when it likes something it will try to move towards it. So your bird will perform a behavior because it desires the *results* of that behavior.

◁ *The preening of feathers is an instinctive behavior but the technique is improved by experience as the bird learns how to use its beak with its tongue.*

▷ *The half-closed eye with the beak partly hidden in raised facial feathers shows this bird to be tired; he'd like to take a nap.*

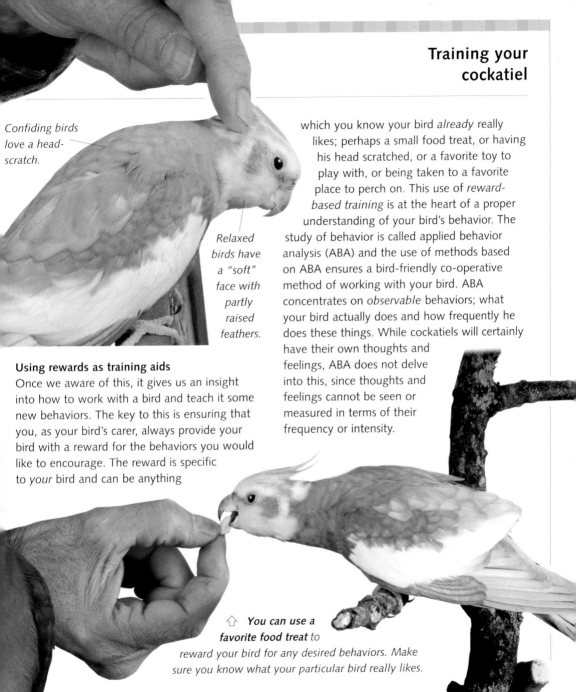

Confiding birds love a head-scratch.

Relaxed birds have a "soft" face with partly raised feathers.

which you know your bird *already* really likes; perhaps a small food treat, or having his head scratched, or a favorite toy to play with, or being taken to a favorite place to perch on. This use of *reward-based training* is at the heart of a proper understanding of your bird's behavior. The study of behavior is called applied behavior analysis (ABA) and the use of methods based on ABA ensures a bird-friendly co-operative method of working with your bird. ABA concentrates on *observable* behaviors; what your bird actually does and how frequently he does these things. While cockatiels will certainly have their own thoughts and feelings, ABA does not delve into this, since thoughts and feelings cannot be seen or measured in terms of their frequency or intensity.

Using rewards as training aids

Once we aware of this, it gives us an insight into how to work with a bird and teach it some new behaviors. The key to this is ensuring that you, as your bird's carer, always provide your bird with a reward for the behaviors you would like to encourage. The reward is specific to *your* bird and can be anything

⇧ **You can use a favorite food treat** to reward your bird for any desired behaviors. Make sure you know what your particular bird really likes.

Training nervous birds

The degree of tameness and confidence that a bird displays depends on many things, including how the bird has been treated in the past. While most cockatiels are quite easy-going, confident birds, some can be nervous or shy. Nervous birds require special care before and during training. Often such nervousness is due to the bird having been handled roughly in the

⇧ **When a caged bird** sees something that causes it to be fearful, it cannot move away from the problem. This effect of being trapped can make a bird nervous and needs to be guarded against.

past – he will remember this experience for a long time. If a bird has been wing-clipped, this can also make it more nervous and these birds may be extremely wary of people, particularly their hands. This nervousness may be made worse by the bird being trapped in a cage unable to get away from fearful things that are happening near it.

Before attempting to ask a nervous bird to step up onto the hand, you will need to go through a gentle taming process which may take several weeks. The same principles of rewarding desired behaviors are used as in the more formal training sessions, but progress with nervous birds may be slow. These birds should always have a perch in their cage which is high enough to allow them to be above your eye-level when you are standing by the cage. This

⇧ **Sitting below a nervous bird** *helps to gain its confidence (**1**). Offer a food treat as a reward when it approaches you (**2**). Later, offer this at the open cage door (**3**). Your patience should be rewarded as even a nervous bird will learn to step up (**4**).*

will reduce the bird's fear of people who might come too close.

Steps to gain a bird's confidence

Start the taming process by sitting down below the bird while it is in its cage but not so close that it shows any signs of nervousness. Sit side-on to the bird and avoid looking directly at it. Let the bird see you doing something such as reading, or having a snack to eat. Keep these sessions quite short at first, just two or three minutes long, but extend them as the bird gets used to you and gradually sit closer to the bird so long as this does not make him nervous. After a few sessions the bird's confidence should improve, and he may become interested in any food you may be eating. At this point, offer the bird a tidbit through the bars of the cage.

At later sessions, try opening the cage door and offer a food treat directly to the bird while he is still in the cage. Just place your handheld tidbit below his beak, provided he appears likely to accept this. Later still, try leaving the cage door open and offer a treat after the bird has come out or has just moved towards the open cage door. To get him to return, place a treat in his food bowl to tempt him back in. Always proceed at a pace that is comfortable for the bird. Use softly spoken words of encouragement as you make progress in this taming stage.

What pet cockatiels need to

So that your bird can spend as much time as possible out of the cage with you and your family, you'll need to teach him to accept a few simple requests or commands from you and other members of your household who wish to interact with him. Once trained to accept these requests, you will be able to ask your bird to fly to and from you, or leave certain places by using a verbal request. This allows you to have good control of your bird while he is out with you and means he will be easy to supervise. In most cases using reward-based training methods, a bird can be taught these requests in five to ten days. It is suggested you teach your bird the following requests in the order below.

STEP UP: This means step up onto my hand please.

GO DOWN: This means please step off my hand onto another perch.

STAY: This means please do not come to me for the moment.

Assuming your bird can fly, make sure that you teach these next requests as well:

GO: This means fly off me and go to another place (perhaps the stand or the cage).

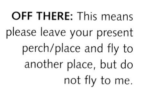

ON HERE: This means please fly to me now.

OFF THERE: This means please leave your present perch/place and fly to another place, but do not fly to me.

Where should you train your bird?
In most cases, you can train your bird in the same room as the cage. However, if your bird is excitable around the cage, it may be easier to teach the first requests to step on and off your hand away from the cage or in another room. You'll need to have some way of getting your (untrained) bird to another room. In most cases, you can wheel the cage in to the other room, encourage the bird to leave the cage, then remove the cage before starting the training session. Nervous birds should always be taught in the same room as their cage. It is best to

⇧ **Most cockatiels** should be trained in the same room as their cage.

⇦ **With an excitable bird,** removing the cage before starting to train can help.

⇧ **Breakable ornaments** should be removed from the room before training the bird.

chair is usually ideal. If this is the first time the bird is to be loose in the room, you should remove any objects or ornaments that he may try to land on.

It's best to position the bird so that he can grip your finger and face you.

arrange things so that the bird is asked to step up and down from places which are between waist and chest height, so the back of a

Note the thumb, held down.

The first requests: stepping up

Since you'll be using reward-based training, you first need to know how you are going to *reward your bird's good behavior* during these sessions. You need to use something which you know your bird already really likes as this provides the bird with the essential motivation for working with you. The reward may be a favorite food treat, or a particular toy, or having his head scratched. It's more effective

⇧ **Before being trained,** *this bird is being tested to determine his favorite food treat. Similar-sized samples of several foods are offered together, to see which he really chooses on each occasion.*

to make sure that on training days the bird only gets these rewards by actually *earning* them: they should not be given for free, otherwise the bird has little incentive to cooperate. Most training sessions should only last for between two to four minutes.

Beginning with step up

Start by having your bird perched on the back of a chair and make sure he is calm but attentive. If the reward is a toy or food treat, you can show him this as you hold it in one hand. Say your bird's name and try to make eyecontact, then approach him and place your other hand just above his feet and say "Step up." Your *step up* hand should be held with your four fingers in line and your thumb down out of the way. You can touch the bird just above his feet with this hand as you say "Step up." Repeat your request if needed and make sure that the bird can see the reward being offered. When he does step up, praise him enthusiastically, then after only a second or two, say *go down* and return him to the chair back and give him his reward, with more verbal praise.

Allow your bird plenty of time to appreciate the reward. Repeat this once or twice more, then end the training session.

It's best just to have one training session on the first day and try to end this on a good point, even if the bird has only stepped up and down once and had his reward. On subsequent days you could schedule two or three sessions, but try to work with your bird when you know he is in a good, calm, and receptive mood. Whatever the bird does during these sessions, make sure you remain completely calm and appear confident. A calm atmosphere will greatly assist your bird in learning the requests. Soon, he should be stepping up and down more easily as he gets used to these sessions.

STEPPING UP

⬆ **Step 1:** *Offer the bird your step-up hand while the reward is visible in your other hand and you clearly say "Step up."*

⬆ **Step 2:** *Keep your step-up hand* **completely still** *as the bird comes on to you; if you wobble or hesitate, the bird will be confused.*

⬆ **Step 3:** *Either give the reward now, or set the bird back down and then give it, but give him time to enjoy it.*

STEPPING DOWN

⬆ **Step 1:** *When asking the bird to step down, your hand should be a bit lower than the target perch he just stepped up from.*

⬆ **Step 2:** *Make the request to go down and gently encourage the bird to step off you onto the perch on which he is to stand.*

⬆ **Step 3:** *Reward and praise your bird for all his efforts. Suitably rewarded birds learn new things very quickly.*

The *stay* and *go* requests

The *stay* request does not mean a bird should stay exactly where it is, but is simply used to ask a bird to refrain from coming to you for the moment, perhaps when you might need to leave the room without the bird following you. If the bird is approaching you and you do not wish him to step onto you or fly to you, just hold your hand with your palm facing the bird and say "Stay." If the bird stops, praise and reward him. If he still tries to come to you, use your hand in this same gesture to block his approach, whether he is walking to you or flying to you. A flying bird will soon learn to turn around and land elsewhere.

When he does land, praise and reward him as usual. This *stay* request is very useful when other people are nervous of interacting with a bird. If other people (perhaps visitors) are not confident around birds, make sure that they use this *stay* request to stop the cockatiel from approaching them.

Teaching *go*

This is the first flight request to teach your bird. This request is used to ask a bird to leave you by flying from you. Initially, teach this request by standing with the bird perched on your hand, about 3 to 4ft (1m) from its cage or any other place he is already used to perching on. Have a reward for the bird conspicuously in view at the place to which you will be asking him to fly. Turn your hand at the wrist so the bird is facing *away from you and towards the familiar perch with the reward in view.* At the same time, use your other hand, held lower down, to point to

the place to which you want the bird to fly, then say "Go, go" and swing the hand with the bird on gently but decisively in the direction you'd like him to go.

Always reward and praise the bird

The bird should leave you and land on the perch/cage top. As soon as he does, *praise him as he takes his reward.* When he is happy to fly from this short distance, gradually increase the distance to the perch. Then practice this request in other locations, until you can ask the bird to leave you wherever you happen to be. If after giving the *go* request, the bird flies off you but tries to land back on you, just use the *stay* request to prevent this.

⇧ *Step 1: Use your free hand to point to the perch; turn your other hand away and give the go request.*

Training your cockatiel

⇩ **With most birds** it doesn't take long for them to learn the stay request and understand that sometimes they cannot fly to you.

⇧ **This is the gesture** to use to ask a bird to refrain from approaching you for the moment. Just have your palm facing the bird as you say "Stay."

Prevent the bird from landing on you.

⇧ **Step 2:** You can move your hand towards the perch and the bird should leave and fly to it.

⇧ **Step 3:** As he lands, praise him and leave him to enjoy his reward for a few moments.

On here and off there

*O*n here is a recall request, asking your bird to fly to you. This is much easier if the bird is already flying to you spontaneously, but it can be taught after the above requests have been accepted. If your bird is already flying to you, you should start to associate this with a verbal cue. So, when your bird appears about to fly to you anyway, hold out your hand for him to land on and give your request of "On here" and reward and praise him enthusiastically when he lands on you. If your bird does not already fly to you spontaneously, you will need a powerful reward to ask him to do so, so make sure you have this first (see page 56 for testing for preferred rewards).

Place the bird on a familiar perch and stand about 3 to 4ft (1m) from him with your arm held out. Hold your food treat or other reward conspicuously in view as well. Your outstretched arm should be a little higher than the perch your bird is on, as birds prefer to fly *up* rather than down when coming to you. Say your bird's name and then say "On here" a few times. As the bird comes, stay completely still until he has landed and give him the reward, together with enthusiastic praise as soon as he lands on you. Allow him plenty of time to enjoy the reward. If the bird does not come after a few attempts of this, avoid your bird becoming bored by taking a break and try again later. Once he is flying to you from a short distance, gradually increase this at later sessions.

The *off there* request

This is generally used as a safety request whereby you ask your bird to leave somewhere

ON HERE

⇧ **Step 1:** For the first few sessions, only stand a few feet away, until the bird gains confidence in flying to you.

⇧ **Step 2:** Call the bird's name, show the reward prominently, and say "On here."

he should not have access to. So if a bird ever lands on an unsafe place, such as an electrical appliance or perhaps a curtain rod, you can use this request to ask him to leave.

In practice you cannot teach this request predictably. However, when your bird does land somewhere that is unsafe or unsuitable, just approach him and say "Off there" as you wave one or both hands at him in an unfamiliar gesture. A wafting motion is often quite effective. You can also wave some harmless object, such as a handkerchief, near the bird. When he leaves, make sure he does not try to land on you, but lands on an appropriate perch, such as his stand or cage and praise him for his cooperation.

OFF THERE
Use a clear hand signal and say 'Off there'.

⬦ ⬆ **When your bird first lands** *on an unsuitable perch, use the* off there *request to ask it to leave. Prompt action should prevent the bird assuming that it can land on these places again.*

⬆ **Step 3:** *Remain perfectly still as the bird comes in to land; this is very important when you begin.*

⬆ **Step 4:** *Give your reward immediately and praise the bird for his efforts at the same time.*

Further training hints

It should not generally be necessary to restrain a bird against its will. However, there will be times when this may be needed. You may need to administer medication or take your bird to a vet or remove him quickly from some dangerous situation. It is best to accustom the bird to what is expected before such needs actually arise.

There are two ways in which to restrain a bird safely. The first involves asking the bird to go down on your chest. To do this, have the bird perched on your hand as usual, but *facing you*, and place your other hand over the bird's back as you say "Go down" and draw the bird to your chest while you withdraw the hand he was perched on. The bird will grip your clothing as he lets go of your hand. Praise the bird and reward him with a gentle head scratch using your free hand. You can then carry the bird in this way as you leave the area and put him down elsewhere, saying "Go down" as you do so. It's useful to practice this request and set the bird down on various *familiar* places before using this method to return a bird to its cage. By this means, the bird won't associate it with having to go back to the cage and this will make such a request easier to use when you might need to put the bird in the cage without delay.

Careful use of a towel
The second method involves the use of a towel, but this should not be confused with the practice of *forcibly* wrapping a bird up in a towel to train or tame it. Such enforced towelling is not appropriate at all. However, it is useful to get your bird used to being held gently in a towel as this makes it easier for birds to be checked by a vet. Once the bird is trained in the requests as explained earlier, you can practice holding him in a towel. Use a towel of a bland or neutral color, such as white or cream, as dark or bold-coloured towels may frighten your bird.

To gradually introduce the bird to the towel, start with the bird on your lap and offer him the corner of the towel to play with or to chew on. After a few sessions, conducted over several days if necessary, let more of the towel come into contact with the bird's body. Eventually you should be able to accustom the bird to being held gently in the towel where you can restrain him for a few minutes. Reward and encourage him at all times by giving praise, head scratches, or some other reward he already really likes.

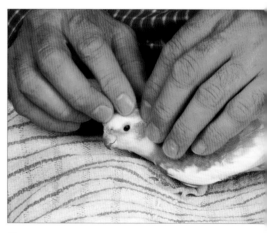

⬆ **With the bird on your lap**, encourage him to become accustomed to the towel over several sessions. Initially he may like to chew a corner of it.

⬇ **At this point,** as the bird's chest just touches your body, say "Go down." His back should be covered by your hand.

⬆ **With the bird perched** on your hand, bring him gently towards your upper body as you place your free hand quietly over his back.

⬆ ⮕ **As the bird's feet** grip your clothing, remove the perching hand and hold him gently against your chest.

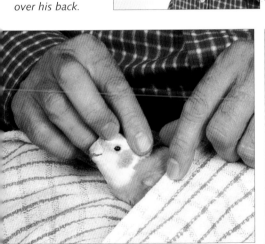

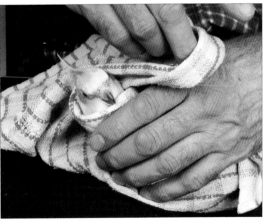

⬆ **Gradually let more** of the towel come into contact with the bird's body as you reward his compliance. This bird enjoys a head scratch.

⬆ **Eventually you should be able** to keep the bird quite calm as you wrap him up carefully in the towel without him struggling or trying to bite to you.

CHAPTER 9

Some frequently asked question

This section looks at some frequently asked questions about cockatiel care.

■ Should I get another (second) bird?

This question is usually asked for two reasons. Either the first bird has bonded to one person only in the family and other family members would like another bird which can be "theirs." Or the bird's main caregiver does not have the same amount of time to spend with the first bird as previously, and considers getting another one as company for the first bird. The matter of acquiring a second bird should not be gone into lightly. There are many issues to consider before

Budgerigars and cockatiels ⇨ *will get on well with each other in most cases.*

doing this. What sort of bird would you get, would it be the same species or a different one? What age should your second bird be, an immature one or an adult? Will the second bird just pair up with your first bird? If it does, will it want anything to do with you or anyone else, or will it reject human companionship? Will it even become aggressive to you or others if it pairs up with the other bird?

Trying to predict the outcomes to these issues is very difficult but some things are more predictable than others. Where you have two adult birds of the

The adult male (right) tells this younger bird to leave.

Such disputes are usually harmless as a young bird grows up...

...but introduce new birds to each other with care.

enjoy the companionship of the first bird. However, these are not predictable outcomes. If you do decide to get a second bird and want to ensure that both birds appreciate human company as companion animals, you could try getting another female cockatiel if you already have a female or try another species, such as a budgie, small parrot or parakeet. You should be able to keep two female cockatiels in the same cage, but it is best to keep any other species in its own cage while in the same room as your cockatiel.

Another parrot can be company for your cockatiel, but should have its own cage.

Meyer's parrot

⇧ **Adult cockatiels will readily** pair up with a companion bird of the opposite sex.

same species and opposite sex they are very likely to pair up. This means they may prefer each other's company to yours. Cockatiels are not aggressive birds so even if they do pair up, they are not likely to reject you by biting, but this can sometimes happen. However, if a second bird is not a closely related species to the first one, the birds are less likely to pair up fully with each other, so you should still

Talking skills and houseplants

■ When will my bird start to talk?

Cockatiels that enjoy a lot of human company, as opposed to living only with other birds, are more likely to talk. While most cockatiels talk as a form of mimicry only, it may be possible to teach your bird to use human speech in its

Many cockatiels can mimic human speech. But by teaching the bird to associate certain objects with the right words, they can learn contextual skills.

⇩ ***Using the right word*** *for an object offered to your bird can encourage speech.*

proper context. When a bird is taught to use speech in context, then your bird may well learn to associate spoken words with the objects and events in question. To do this, the bird is taught to use speech in much the same way as you would encourage a human baby to

start to learn to talk. So repeating a word or phrase clearly, in association with particular events or with objects that are given to the bird, may result in the bird using these words in their proper context.

Some cockatiels do learn to talk (mimic) within their first few months of life and many pet cockatiels manage to talk by two years of age; but some never talk at all. There does not seem to be any difference between the talking abilities of the different colour mutations.

◌ ***Birds kept indoors*** *and receiving plenty of attention are more likely to reproduce human speech.*

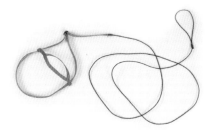

■ Can I use a harness so that I can safely take my bird outdoors?

No type of leg restraint can be used on these birds as this can cause the leg to be dislocated. Most cockatiels also dislike anything touching their feathers and this causes them to react badly to wearing anything, including a body harness. So it is not recommended that you try to fit one on your bird. The best way to give your bird some outdoor flying time is to provide him with a day flight or aviary.

■ Are any houseplants unsafe for birds?

Very few plants are harmful to birds and there are far too many houseplants available commercially to list species as safe or unsafe here. Some plants which are known to be unsafe for humans or other mammals, such as yew for instance, can be

⇧ *In most cases, houseplants* are not harmful to birds. If you are not sure of a plant's safety, ask for advice at the shop where you bought it or remove it from the room in which you keep your birds.

eaten safely by some birds. However, the fact remains that there is no definitive list of bird-safe plants which has actually been tested on parrot-like birds. If you have any concerns, it's best to ask advice from the shop where you bought the plants. If a plant is listed as unsafe (for human consumption), it is sensible to err on the safe side and assume that it is also potentially harmful for birds.

Wing clipping

■ Should my cockatiel have its wings clipped?
Most people prefer to keep their bird without clipping its wings and this is strongly recommended. The proponents of clipping maintain that it is safer for the bird, but this is not necessarily the case. All birds are subject to some risks, whether they are clipped or not: clipped birds are just vulnerable to different types of risk than a full winged bird. If clipped birds escape, there is more chance of them being caught by a dog or cat or being run over by a vehicle. Other problems for clipped birds can also be serious. Where clipping prevents upward flight, such birds often become very fearful

◻ *This is a light clip where seven primaries are cut. If this were done to both this bird's wings, it would reduce the bird's flying abilities, but still allow it to land safely.*

How a typical clipped wing would look.

⇩ *This bird has been badly clipped and is at risk of injury. Imping would restore flying ability.*

or phobic and generally have greatly reduced confidence. A cockatiel's most important means of escaping from a fearful situation is, of course, to simply fly away, preferably to a higher perch. Again, clipping denies the bird this most vital escape mechanism. Cockatiels have no behavioral response to cope with being unable to fly and many find flightlessness very distressing.

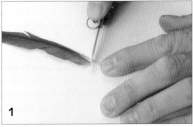

◁ *Repairing by imping: (1) The donor feather(s) are prepared by cutting off about one inch of the shaft. (2) A small splint is inserted half-way into the shaft of the donor feather and glued in. (3) This splinted feather is attached to the bird's remaining clipped feather stump. (4) Done properly, the donor feathers are as good as the bird's own.*

When clipping is done, it can be performed in many different ways and some types of clip are more severe than others. Generally, some or all of the bird's main flight feathers (the ten primary feathers) are clipped short. Usually this is done to both wings, so that the bird retains some balance and can recover from a fall without injuring itself. A one-wing clip would deliberately unbalance the bird and can cause serious risk of injury or death.

The benefits of imping feathers

If you acquire a clipped bird, the molting process should eventually see a regrowth of any clipped feathers. However, regrowing the feathers is a long process (two to three months) and clipped birds often damage the growing feathers which can bleed profusely. This problem can be prevented by having an avian vet repair your bird's clipped wings by splinting on (imping) donor feathers which have been molted by another cockatiel (see above).

Clipping is sometimes justified in order to control a bird's movements. But the training section in this book explains how you can teach your bird some simple commands to control its flight. This usually only takes a few days and these requests, once taught, give you all the control you need. Of course, your bird can also behave more naturally around you by being able to fly. It is the provision of opportunities for a bird to express its normal daily behaviors, including flight, which is at the heart of the *prevention* of a range of common behavioral problems. So, it is recommended that your bird should not be clipped but be *encouraged* to fly.

Keeping an unclipped bird safe

■ **How should I keep a full-winged bird safely?**
When keeping birds which can fly normally, it is important to follow some common-sense precautions.

Your bird should be properly supervised at all times when it is out of its cage, so make sure that you teach the bird the flight requests explained earlier in the training section.

Be aware of common household dangers. Birds should not be in rooms which have ceiling

fans, open external doors and windows, or large mirrors. Large-pane windows can be very confusing for a bird so these should have curtains or net drapes hung in front of them. Do not allow your bird into the kitchen as there are far too many dangers here for birds, such as unprotected sources of heat and fumes released by hot Teflon-coated pans that are potentially toxic to birds.

Ensure your bird has a range of places outside the cage to use as perches. You may find it easier to manage the bird if these places are no higher than your head – for example, the backs of chairs and sofas, window ledges, and tables. Cockatiels should not just be left to get on with things on their own in any new situation. As highly social creatures, these birds need guidance and encouragement from you. So, when introducing your bird to any new place or new room make sure to show the bird the places you would like him to use as perches. Just ask him to go down onto these places using the requests you have already taught him and reward him on the first few occasions with a tidbit or a favorite small toy to

◁ *The net curtain behind this bird prevents it from flying into the window or crashing into the glass.*

Some frequently asked questions

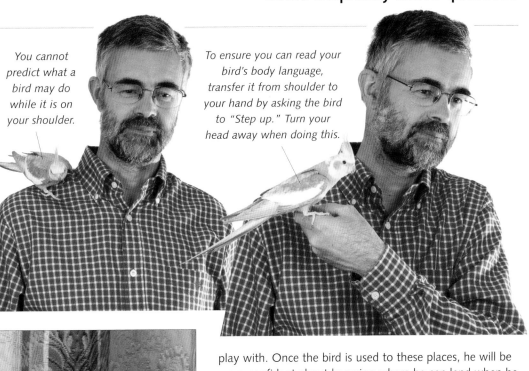

You cannot predict what a bird may do while it is on your shoulder.

To ensure you can read your bird's body language, transfer it from shoulder to your hand by asking the bird to "Step up." Turn your head away when doing this.

play with. Once the bird is used to these places, he will be more confident about knowing where he can land when he does fly. Later, try using the *go* command to ask the bird to fly to these places from your hand.

While it is acceptable for the bird to *land* on your shoulder, the shoulder should not be seen as a normal perch. Always transfer the bird from your shoulder to your hand as soon as he lands there. Just use the *step up* command for this. Your *hand* should be the bird's normal perch when it is on you, not your arm or your shoulder.

◁ **When introducing your bird** to a room, practice setting him down on various suitable places using the *go down* request. Ensure he is rewarded when he steps down.

Health and hygiene

■ Can I toilet train my bird?

While it is certainly possible to get your bird to use certain places to do its droppings, this needs to be done with care. You will soon realize by watching your bird's body language when he needs to go to the toilet. At this point, you can try moving him to one of the places you would like him to use. Then praise him just after he has passed his droppings. It is important to have *several places* which your bird can use, otherwise he may become obsessed with only going to one place and this can cause problems. After a few instances of moving him to these places at the right moment, the bird should get used to this routine and then even make his own way there without your help. Alternatively, many people are quite relaxed about this and instead of toilet training they just clean up promptly as needed using a tissue and a good household cleaning product.

■ How often should the cage be cleaned?

It's best to use old newspapers for covering the cage floor, and these should be changed every day. Once a week the whole cage, including the perches, should be scrubbed clean using a mild, diluted disinfectant and hot water. Some bird supplement suppliers sell bird-safe disinfectant, although other disinfectants are usually safe when diluted. Follow the manufacturer's recommendations regarding the strength of the solution it is advisable to use. Where a roosting box is used, birds rarely soil this, but the box should be cleaned thoroughly, like the cage, once a week. The wood shavings or newspaper lining the box should be replaced once a week.

■ How often should food bowls be cleaned?

Food bowls used for dry seed should be washed once a week. Bowls used for wet foods, such as fruit or vegetables or soaked seeds etc., and the water bowl should be washed clean each day. Again bird supplement suppliers sell bird-safe

⇧ *Cockatiels are much easier to clean up after than larger parrots, and they make much less mess as well, as their food intake is smaller.*

⇦ *Old newspapers are ideal* for lining the cage floor. Food remains, droppings and feather dust tend to accumulate on the cage bars and perches, so these need to be scrubbed clean thoroughly once a week using a mild disinfectant and hot water.

⇧ *Dirty food bowls and dirty water* can harbor germs. Regular cleaning of food and water bowls helps to protect your bird from illnesses.

antiseptic which you may wish to use as well when washing the food pots each day.

■ What about general health and hygiene?
With a common-sense approach, healthy birds pose few health problems for most people.

However, care should be taken to avoid a bird's droppings contaminating anywhere where human food might be prepared; so it's best to prevent birds having access to these areas, particularly in households with young children or elderly people, whose immune systems may not be as strong as other people's. In rare cases a disease called psittacosis may be transmitted to humans through inhalation of dust contaminated with infected particles in droppings. If you are ever ill and need to visit your doctor, always state that you keep birds in case this is relevant. If you think your bird is actually passing psittacosis in its droppings then the bird needs to be seen by a vet immediately for treatment. Fortunately psittacosis is rarely seen in humans but a far more common problem is people's allergy to feather dust.

Remember to wash your hands before preparing your bird's food. Birds are sensitive to many common household chemicals so make sure your hands are clean and uncontaminated before handling any food or the bird.

Beak and claw care

■ Do I need to trim my bird's claws?
In order to be able to grip perches and many other surfaces properly, cockatiels need fairly sharp claws. These birds are very vulnerable to

night frights anyway (see page 77) and if a bird has blunt claws, it is liable to slip off some perches or even fall and crash land. In most cases, therefore, it is not necessary to trim a bird's claws regularly; they will only need

⇧ **You can fit an abrasive perch** with a diameter of about 0.5in (12mm), low down in the cage, where the bird will use it from time to time.

checking occasionally and trimming if really overgrown. In the wild, the bird's claws wear down and they are naturally kept at the right length. In captivity, since the bird is much less

⇧ **Using a nail-file** or similar abrasive material for trimming claws is safer than using nail clippers as there is less risk of accidentally causing bleeding.

active, some excessive growth may occur and cause the bird problems, so you will then need to trim the claws, or have a bird vet trim them.

Rather than using clippers for this, it is best to use a small file, nail-file or fine abrasive material to simply file off any excess growth while a helper holds the bird carefully wrapped in a towel. Alternatively, you can also use an abrasive perch in your bird's cage, so your bird's claws get some wear each time the perch is used. However, cockatiels should not be required to use an abrasive perch for long periods as this can cause some discomfort. Accordingly the perch should not be a favorite or top perch, but one lower down in the cage, perhaps beside a food or water bowl.

■ Do I need to trim my bird's beak?

It is not recommended that you ever try to trim your bird's beak. Like the claws, the beak needs to be sharp so the bird can eat normally. The beak will only need to receive attention if it is genuinely overgrown and causing the bird some difficulty in eating. Even then, trimming should only be done by a specialist avian vet.

■ Should I let a bird take food from my mouth?

It is recommended that you do not allow your bird to take food from your mouth. Our mouths

⇦ *Cockatiels are adept at testing anything they can get their beaks into, including buttons!*

⇧ *The bird must have a sharp point to the beak to enable it to split open seeds.*

and the mouths of birds both contain many different types of bacteria and you should not put yourself or your bird at risk of possibly contaminating one another in this way. Many people have had their lips bitten when doing this and this injury can require a visit to hospital for first-aid treatment.

Holiday care and night-frights

■ What should I do when I go on holiday?
If you have recently acquired a young bird, he or she will be very dependent on you, so you should simply *not go away at all* until the bird is about a year old. To a very young bird, the sudden departure of its main companion can be extremely stressful. Under such circumstances, the bird may become distressed and start to pluck its own feathers out. In the wild, the bird's parents would not desert their young, and immature birds have no behavioral adaptation to cope with such a loss. With older birds, it is best to ensure they are used to the person who is going to care for them

Cover the cage with a cloth during transit.

⇧ **To get your bird used** to going into a traveling cage, always offer a favorite tidbit as a reward when the bird obediently goes inside.

⇧ **If you go on holiday,** try to find someone to care for your cockatiel who already knows the bird and is thoroughly familiar with his needs.

while you are away. The holiday sitter should be familiar with the bird's needs and be able to handle the bird in a similar way to you. Provided the bird is out of the cage for some time each day and relates reasonably well to the sitter, and other aspects of his care such as food and caging remain the same, the bird should cope with your temporary absence. Some small animal boarding places do take parrots in as well, but you may feel more confident in the knowledge that your bird is with someone you already know and trust in the security of your own home.

Some frequently asked questions

■ I've heard about cockatiels and night-frights. What does this mean?

Cockatiels are very vulnerable to what appear to be panic attacks at night. This is more common with aviary birds, but it can happen with caged birds as well. Normally something causes the birds to be extremely fearful and they make frantic efforts to fly away from the apparent problem. Sudden noises or anything which reminds them of a predator may cause a panic reaction. Wild cockatiels will fly at night, but of course there are no cage bars to injure them, so this behavior is normal when they feel threatened by something. The best way to prevent it is to supply low-wattage lighting, no brighter than moonlight, for the birds overnight. This night light should be placed so that no moving shadows are cast by it should anyone move around in the room. This allows your bird to see things and reduces incidences of crashing into the cage bars. You should not approach a bird while it is panicking, as it may associate you with the problem and become extremely fearful of you. Just stay well back and talk to the bird without handling it until it calms down.

⇧ *A fairly dim light, left on overnight near the cage, may help reduce attacks of night-fright. This should not cast any shadows the bird might see.*

⇧ *Some birds prefer their cages to be covered at night with a towel or blanket, and this also reduces the chances of night-fright or panic attacks.*

CHAPTER 10

Maturing birds and biting

Growing up: from baby to adult.

As with other captive animals, cockatiels should never be blamed for whatever they do, nor is it helpful to project *human* emotions and values

⇧ *Though less tame initially,* baby birds raised by their own parents tend to make better pets than those which have been hand reared.

onto birds. All the behaviors you see your bird performing are done because the bird is either trying to obtain something it needs, or it is trying to avoid something which may be harmful to it. As a young

⇨ *Cockatiels do squabble* from time to time, but they rarely hurt each other. Where aggression occurs, it tends to amount to a lot of noise rather than actual physical harm.

cockatiel begins to mature at around 6 to 12 months, you will see some changes in its behavior, much as you would expect to see in any other animal, such as a puppy or a kitten as it grows up. The cuddly tame baby bird on sale at a breeder's premises or a pet shop may well remain very affectionate later in life, but most birds naturally become more assertive on maturity. The submissive behaviors seen in young birds are an adaptation that encourage others to treat them gently while they are defenceless. But as the bird matures, its needs change, so naturally does its behavior. To be prepared for your bird's generally more assertive, adult behaviors just follow the training suggestions explained earlier, and accept the changes in your bird as it becomes an adult.

Common behavioral problems

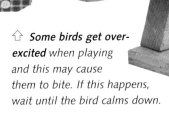

biting can occur. It is important not to over-react if this does happen, otherwise the birds will remain over-excited and the biting behavior may become reinforced by your reactions. Biting often first occurs with birds as they begin to mature and the first incidents are commonly caused by the bird simply being over-excited, perhaps while in a playful mood. So, try to interact with your bird in ways that do not result in such over-excitement.

⇧ **Some birds get over-excited** when playing and this may cause them to bite. If this happens, wait until the bird calms down.

Biting behavior

What makes cockatiels so endearing as companion birds is their very social, indeed non-aggressive, nature. When treated with care they are sensitive, friendly birds. However, sometimes

If you are bitten hard, do not return the bird to its cage, otherwise you will soon have difficulty in doing even that! The most effective response is simply to turn your back on the bird and put your hands out of the bird's sight for a few moments. You can also walk out of the room, closing the door behind you *(right)* and stay out for two or three minutes. When you return, wait for the bird to interact with you, and carry on as normal. If biting occurs again, remain calm and repeat this tactic of leaving the bird alone for a few minutes to allow it time to calm down. In most cases the bird soon makes the connection between biting and being left on its own and then it has an incentive to cease biting because it does not want to lose your companionship.

⇧ **A cockatiel's bite** is not usually painful, nor will it draw blood unless the bird is very upset or angry.

Dealing with self-plucking

Cockatiels are not as vulnerable to self-plucking as some other parrot-like birds, but some do suffer from this condition. Self-plucking does not occur in the wild; it only happens to captive birds. Contributing causes may include the bird's diet or medical problems so have your bird examined by a specialist avian vet if he starts to damage his own feathers. However, there is increasing evidence that it is the frustration of natural daily behaviors that appear to be the main cause of self-plucking. Cockatiels

that are most vulnerable to self-plucking usually experience the conditions described below:

They are solitary pet birds who are (or were) wing-clipped; they have been hand reared, not parent raised; they spend long periods during the day in their cages rather than being out of the cage, interacting with their companions or other birds; they also have little or no opportunities to fly and, most importantly, no opportunities to actually forage for some of their food.

Encourage foraging behaviors
Wild cockatiels spend many hours each day just finding their food and they are "programmed" to carry out these foraging behaviors. But captive birds have food available at all times a few inches from their beaks and are prone to suffer severe boredom. It is the frustration of being unable to perform their foraging

⇧ **This bird, kept in a barren cage,** is at serious risk of self-plucking and other behavioural problems.

⇧ **A foraging toy: spread a few seeds** on a small piece of newspaper and roll this up.

⇨ **What cockatiels do naturally!**
Rummaging about for some favourite seeds in a sand-tray.

behaviors in captivity which causes so many behavioral problems. To prevent and help cure self-plucking, it is necessary to keep the bird busy and occupied during the daytime. The bird should have a range of toys which he actually plays with and these should include puzzle toys in which food can be hidden. These are available from good pet stores but you can make your own inexpensive versions.

Hidden food treats
Try hiding some seeds in a small cardboard tube filled with newspaper, or a tidbit inside a small cardboard box. Food hung up in small baskets or in bird-feeders used for wild birds can also be used. Cockatiels feed on the ground so give your bird the chance to hunt for food treats by use of a foraging tray. This is a tray of sand or fine gravel with some seeds sprinkled on it for your bird to pick out. Give plenty of time for your bird to fly, either indoors or in an aviary used as a daytime flight. The key thing is to keep your bird's beak and brain busy with other objects. With plenty of out-of-cage time and lots of things to chew up, your bird is much less likely to chew on his own feathers.

⇧ **Twist it** so the seeds are wrapped tightly.

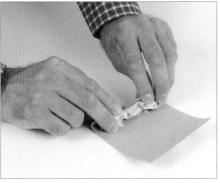

⇧ **Roll this up** in a piece of thin card; the bird has to work harder to get the seeds.

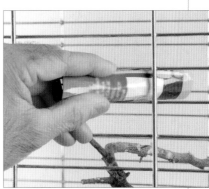

⇧ **Wedge this in the cage** bars. You can make several at a time.

Nervous and phobic cockatiels

Cockatiels are more vulnerable to panic attacks (night frights) than most pet birds and those who cannot fly, perhaps because they are wing-clipped, are even more susceptible to nervousness. Phobic birds show an exaggerated fear of certain actions, objects or people. Sometimes, the fear is so great the bird may thrash around in its cage. This behavior has nothing to do with aggression: it means the bird is in real fear of its life. You should remove the source of your bird's fear *immediately*, even if

⇦ *If cockatiels are kept on their own, or with wings clipped, they may be more nervous. As wild birds, cockatiels gain a great deal confidence simply by living within a flock of their own kind.*

⇦ *A bird's confidence is more likely to improve if it has some perches above your eye level.*

the source is you! Just walk away, even leave the room, but do so immediately. Make sure your bird has a perch in the cage which is above your eye level. This helps to reduce the bird's fear of people who come close. Birds do not show any evidence of being able to accept reassurance as humans do, so if the bird is afraid

Getting a bird to overcome its nervousness has to be done at a pace which is comfortable for the bird. For more advice see the section on night frights (page 77) and follow the guidelines there. Getting a bird to calm down and resume its former tame condition following some fearful event can take time. You'll need to be patient and work slowly and carefully with the bird,

⇧ **Cockatiels have long memories** if something goes wrong and upsets them. A careful, patient approach is the way to win back your bird's trust.

⇧ **If a bird lands badly,** do not approach it at once. Always wait until the bird has collected his senses before going anywhere near him.

of you or something you have done, attempts at reassurance are pointless and can even make a bad situation much worse.

Don't make a crash landing any worse!
If your bird crash lands somewhere and this is followed by you approaching him to reassure him, he may associate you with any pain or fear that he is feeling at this moment, and begin to fear you as part of the cause of his pain. In this situation, remove yourself from the bird until he has collected his senses and has had time to calm down.

using whatever rewards you know the bird is likely to accept. If other people can work with the bird better than you, then give them the opportunity to do so at first. You can then help at a later time when the bird's confidence is showing some signs of returning.

Egg laying and noise problems

Egg laying

Female cockatiels are well-known for their egg laying, even as solitary caged birds. Many female cockatiels lay several eggs regularly in their cages. The production of eggs puts a great strain on a bird and should be minimized. Females are inclined to try to lay a full clutch of four (but this can be up to seven) eggs before they cease laying. She may then try to incubate the eggs for about three weeks. On no account should any eggs be removed from the bird, otherwise she will be stimulated to lay even more to replace her "stolen" eggs. Leave the eggs with her until she ceases to be interested in them or they break up and disintegrate.

To reduce further egg laying, once her first egg has been laid it can help to provide her with dummy eggs. This gives her the feel of a full clutch underneath her. Supply up to four more dummies; these can be anything which is about the same size and colour as her small white eggs. Egg-laying

⇨ *The provision of dummy eggs can induce the bird to feel that she has a full clutch; this can help to prevent even more eggs from being laid.*

⇧ *Egg-laying birds must have adequate calcium and vitamin D3. This can be added to the drinking water or to moist foods as a supplement.*

cockatiels will need extra calcium in their diet. This is best supplied as a liquid supplement from bird supplement suppliers and is given either in the drinking water or with wet foods; just follow the manufacturer's instructions regarding the dosage.

Problems with noise

Unlike most other parrots, cockatiels are not usually noisy birds. However, if the bird does start to make a loud repetitive sound, this is usually due to a lack of attention and boredom. Birds that spend too long in their cages will be prone to this behavior, so they just need to be allowed out more and be kept occupied.

Common behavioral problems

If a bird enjoys plenty of time out of the cage, but nevertheless starts to make a loud noise that causes a problem, it is vital that you do not inadvertently reward the bird by giving him any attention, including saying "No" to him. The most effective solution to such a noise problem is for you, and everyone else, to simply leave the room each time your

Boredom can result in loud calls.

⇧ **Trying to reprimand** a noisy bird is likely to make the problem even worse. Leaving the room is generally more effective.

◁ **Some noise should be** accepted as part of the bird's normal behavior.

bird starts to produce the unwanted noise. Eventually, most birds realize that their behavior has caused you to leave and when they make this connection, they have an incentive to stop making the unwanted noise.

CHAPTER 11

First aid and health care

Providing your bird has a good diet, plenty of time each day out of the cage to exercise by flying and a stimulating environment with a good relationship with its keepers, it should stay physically and mentally healthy. However, you should be prepared for the possibility of illness long before it occurs by taking the trouble to find a good specialist bird vet. It is important to use a vet who has considerable experience of treating birds, rather than an ordinary practitioner whose skills may not include avian medicine. It is also recommended that your bird should be examined at least once a year for a general health check-up. Most bird vets are members of the Association of Avian Vets and various websites list their contact details. Bird vets are also listed in *Parrots* magazine each month. Some parts of the country have several bird vets, but in other places you may find you are many miles from a bird vet. However, it is worth travelling some distance to secure the services of a good vet.

◁ *There are now a good number* of bird vets, so you should be able to find one not too far away from you.

⇧ *Watch for the first signs* of illness. An inactive bird who seems to be off color may need help, so take note of your bird's condition each day.

Veterinary facilities to look out for

Good bird vets will have some or all of the following facilities:

- Anesthesia by isofluorane gas (this is a very safe method of anesthesia for birds).
- Ability to do imping (restoring flight by repairing a bird's wings following any wing clipping).
- Ability to do Complete Blood Count and biochemistry tests.

- Use of an endoscope for internal examinations.
- Ability to take tissue samples (biopsies) for testing.
- Staff who know how to handle parrots correctly, using a towel (not gloves) to minimize stress.
- 24-hour hospitalization facilities for birds.

Take care over contagious diseases

If you do have to treat a sick bird, make sure that you follow your vet's advice about the dose and frequency of administering any medicines, and any other aspects of nursing care that are suggested. If the illness is contagious, you will need to isolate the bird from any other birds you may have until the infection has passed and the vet has said that it is safe to allow the birds to mix together communally again. Birds housed

⇧ *Healthy birds* *have good feather condition and a clean vent with no residue of droppings here.*

together often carry the same illnesses and infections. So if you have one sick bird in a group of birds, seek your vet's advice about any other preventative treatment that your other birds might need to improve their chances of remaining healthy.

⇩ *Regular spraying* *with plain water is vital to maintain good feather condition.*

Keep the sprayer lower than the bird

Set the nozzle to produce a fine mist of droplets.

Recognizing sick birds

Sick birds often appear tired with fluffed up feathers and sunken, dull, or half-closed eyes. They may have difficulty balancing or using a perch and may go to the floor of the cage instead. Sick birds often shows signs of being less aware of things going on around them. The droppings may not be normal, and the bird may not be eating as usual. Sick birds often lose weight and this can be rapid. Make sure you know your bird's *normal weight* and check this from time to time.

Sick birds: what to do

If the bird can be weighed without causing further stress, then do so and write this figure down. Sick birds usually gain great benefit from simply being put somewhere very warm, 79 to 86°F (26 to 30°C) and kept out of bright lights. You can supply heat using a ceramic infrared heat lamp placed above the cage (this only emits heat and no light). Place this so the bird can move away from the lamp if at any time it feels too hot. Use

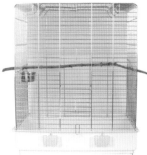

⇩ *This heat-lamp suspended over the cage allows the bird to move in and out of the extra heat at will.*

a thermometer to check the temperature around the cage (but keep this out of reach of the bird). The provision of heat will mean the bird will need to drink regularly, so make sure the bird has easy access to drinking water and wet foods, such as grapes, apples, or lettuce. Once the bird is receiving heat treatment phone your vet, explain the bird's symptoms and get emergency advice without delay. When taking your bird to the vet, keep it very warm all the time.

⇨ *Make sure you know your bird's normal weight. Good quality electric kitchen scales are ideal for the job.*

⇦ **Some of the items** to keep for first aid use. The thermometer is used to measure air temperature near the cage.

Dark towels may frighten the bird.
- Ceramic infrared heat lamp, or a hospital cage.
- Thermometer.
- Small syringes and a bent spoon for giving medicine or food.
- Forceps.
- Pair of small sharp scissors.
- Hand-feeding formula.
- Travelling cage with one securely fitted perch.
- Good quality electric scales.

Stress alone can make things worse for the bird, so always act calmly. Restrict the bird's ability to see out of its carrier during travelling as this also helps to reduce stress.

⇩ **It is often much easier** to give medicine if it is offered reasonably warm from a warm syringe. The very small 1ml syringes are ideal for cockatiels.

Items for your bird's first aid needs:
- Avian vet's contact details.
- Cotton balls and cotton swabs – used to help stop bleeding.
- Styptic pencil (to stop bleeding of claws or damaged beak only).
- Antibiotic ointment to treat wounds.
- Avian-safe antiseptic.
- Electrolyte solution, e.g. Prolyte-C used after other medication has ceased – it aids digestion.
- Avian multivitamin powder.
- Glucose powder – this can be given as an emergency food when dissolved in water.
- Towel – this should be a bland color, such as white or cream.

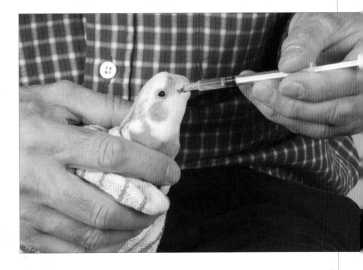

CHAPTER 12

Recovering an escaped bird

Most birds escape through an open door or window. If owners have got into the habit of letting their bird perch on their shoulder (instead of their hand), these birds commonly escape as the companion walks outdoors forgetting that the cockatiel is on their shoulder and the bird flies off. It is best to prevent a bird from using your shoulder as a perch; instead always have the bird on your hand .

Cockatiels fly at about 35mph (56kph) and can be many miles away within a few minutes. So, in the event of an escape, what should you do?

First you should have these items ready on hand:
- A good pair of binoculars.
- Some of your bird's favorite food treats and the food bowl from his cage.

⇩ ⇗ *Many birds escape* when owners *completely forget about the bird on their shoulder as they walk outdoors!*

Cockatiels are agile flyers and the wind can carry them quickly away.

- A travelling case and/or cloth holding bag with drawstrings, to put the bird in if you do catch him.

An escaped bird will find the outdoors very confusing
If a bird has panicked while escaping, it will probably fly a great distance before coming down to land in an exhausted state. However, a bird that escapes while otherwise quite calm usually does not go far and will call loudly trying to find other birds to follow. In this case the bird tends to fly in a wide circle around the point of release, looking for somewhere to land. For most cockatiels that find themselves flying outdoors, everything is confusing simply because it is unfamiliar to the bird and it will be nervous about landing on strange places. Tree branches, which may be blowing in the wind, will frighten the bird and

bare rooftops or TV aerials may also not be acceptable.

Stay calm when you approach the bird

Eventually though the bird will land as it becomes exhausted. Escaped birds often land in the tallest tree in the area and then try to hide by climbing down into the foliage. At this point the bird will be very tense and liable to fly again unless allowed to calm down. In winter when most trees have lost their leaves, you may find the bird by direct searching, using your binoculars, but in summer it can be extremely difficult to spot a cockatiel in a leafy tree. In such a case it's best to rely on your ears to start with by listening out for your bird's calls. Tame pet birds (as opposed to aviary birds) will often respond to the familiar voice of their keeper, so employ your usual calls and whistles as you search for your bird.

Eight or ten times magnification binoculars are ideal.

⇧ ⇨ **Escaped birds commonly end up** *landing in the tallest tree in the area. Remember, you may have more chance of* **hearing** *your bird than seeing it.*

Coaxing an escaped cockatiel

The more people who know about your lost bird, the greater are your chances of someone spotting him and telling you where he has been seen. Make copies of a short note with a picture of your bird, details of when it was lost and your contact details and deliver this to as many people as you can in your neighborhood. When someone sees a strange bird they often contact the police, local radio station, local vets or the ASPCA. So make sure you also contact these organizations with details of your bird.

⬆ *Your chances of recovery are much better if you can make some effort to climb up to the bird.*

⬆ *Escaped cockatiels can actually survive quite well if they find food and shelter within a day or so.*

When you do eventually find your bird, he is likely to be high up in a tree, and he will be nervous of flying down to you. The bird's instincts tell him to stay high up where he'll feel safer. However, a bird will often actually try to *walk* down if you can devise a way of approaching him that offers him a route to you that doesn't require him to fly. Usually this means you'll have to use a ladder and make some attempt to go up towards your bird. Even being a few feet off the ground can be a great help in persuading the bird to come towards you for some of his favorite food. At this point it is best to offer the bird a small tidbit and just stay with him as he eats this to keep him calm.

down

Trained birds are easier to get back

Depending on how the bird is used to being handled, you will have to decide how you are going to secure him. Birds trained to accept the usual requests *will still obey these* even outdoors. So, if you have trained your bird it is quite likely to simply step up when asked, and walk onto your hand. If you are up a tree, you should have a bag or box into which you can put the bird before you climb down. You can make a suitable bag from a small pillowcase. This should have a drawstring and a strap which goes over

A bag is easier to use if you have to climb a tree.

⇦ ⇧ *Exhausted birds will sometimes* end up on the ground. Always act calmly and once you have secured the bird, keep him somewhere where he cannot see what is going on around him.

your shoulder to leave your hands free when coming down the ladder. Alternatively you can lower the bag down using a long line to a colleague who will wait for you to descend.

If you see your bird, but are not able to catch him by nightfall, return to the same place *before light the next morning* and try again. In summer, this will mean getting there before 4am. Most birds do not fly after dark, so he should still be there.

Index

Note: Page numbers set in *italic* type refer to captions to pictures; page numbers set in **bold** type indicate the main subject reference.

Index

Picture Credits

Unless otherwise credited below, all the photographs that appear in this book were
taken by **Neil Sutherland** especially for Interpet Publishing. The publisher would also like to thank Mike Taylor at **Northern Parrots** (www.24Parrot.com) for kindly supplying the pictures of the cage and parrot stand that are credited below.

Mark Cocquio: 11 top right, 35 top.

iStockphoto.com:
Nicholas Belton: 91 bottom right.
Hagit Berkovich: 23 top left.
EuToch: 22, 66-67, 85 top right.
Lee Feldstein: 82 top right.
Susan Flashman: 8.
Christine Gonsalves: 52 left.
Gremlin: 80 left.
Peter Hibberd: 34 centre right, 36 bottom left.
Eric Isselée: 64 top right.
Jerry Koch: 15 top left, 17 top right, 65 top left.
Manuela Krause: 10 bottom right.
Jill Lang: 13 top, 21 centre right.
Mary Morgan: 23 bottom right, 76 bottom left.
NiseriN: 92 top right.
Tomislav Stajduhar: 25 centre right.
Willie B. Thomas: 86 bottom left.
Toya: 14 centre right.
Gary Unwin: 23 top right, 92 centre left.
Scott Winegarden: 12 centre left.

Leanne's Cockatiels: 16 top, 19 top right, 19 bottom left.

Northern Parrots: 39 left, 45 bottom left.

Peter Odekerken: 9 left, 18 bottom left, 18 bottom centre, 19 top centre.

Peter Odekerken/ABK Publications: 6, 9 top centre, 19 bottom right.

Shutterstock Inc.:
Greg Atkinson: 16 bottom.
Katrina Brown: 7 top, 11 bottom left, 13 bottom left, 14 bottom right, 36 top centre, 78 top left, 78 bottom.
Kenneth William Caleno: 10 centre left.
Tabitha Skye Campbell: 41 right.
EuToch: 12 bottom, 25 top centre, 32 centre left, 34 left.
First Class Photos PTY Ltd: 75 centre right, 93 left.
Susan Flashman: 15 bottom right.
Gelpi: 17 top left.
Johanna Goodyear: 17 bottom.
Margo Harrison: 44.
Hernan H. Hernandez: 86 top right.
Nicky Jacobs: 83 right.
Jill Lang: 20 top centre.
Michelle D. Milliman: 13 centre right, 21 left.
Allison Stec: 38 top left.
Beth Van Trees: 68 bottom left.
Michael Weed: 7 bottom.
Ashley Whitworth: 9 bottom right.
Judy Worley: 91 top left.

Published by
Interpet Publishing,
Vincent Lane,
Dorking,
Surrey RH4 3YX,
England

ISBN 978 1 84286 172 1

Editor: **Philip de Ste. Croix**
Designer: **Philip Clucas** MCSD
Photographer: **Neil Sutherland**
Diagram artwork: **Martin Reed**
Index: **Amanda O'Neill**
Production management: **Consortium, Suffolk**
Print production: **Sino Publishing House Ltd, Hong Kong**

Disclaimer

The information and recommendations in this book are given without any guarantees on behalf of the author and publisher, who disclaim any liability with the use of this material.

Acknowledgements

Greg would like to thank Rachel Lewis for her comments on the text. Smokey, Pearl and Dean performed to their usual high standards.
Thanks also to Dan Moss for his kind assistance in loaning Pearl and Dean for photography.